# CONTENTS

# ACKNOWLEDGEMENTS

Prints were received for inclusion from D. W. K. Jones, N. V. Martin, R. Maybray, E. Ogden, R. H. G. Simpson, H. J. Snook and Surfleet Transport Photographs. In addition coloured transparencies were provided by B. Johnson, D. Kaye, P. J. Marshall and M. Rickitt.

# PREFACE

THIS three-volume series of pocket encyclopaedias covers the history of the British bus and trolleybus from their inception until 1968. This volume saw a considerable change from the low-powered, petrol-engined, high-chassised, solid-tyred, open-topped near-cousin of the horse bus and the tramcar to the relatively high-powered, diesel-engined, low-slung, well-sprung, pneumatic-tyred, weather-proofed grandchild, who bears very little resemblance to those models of the Edwardian epoch. This second volume covers the period between the two World Wars; the final six years deal with the effect of the Second World War on the world of the public service vehicle, when for a time it looked as if retrograde steps were being taken (e.g. wooden slatted seats, strictly governed engines, etc.).

The range of vehicles that could be illustrated in the period covered by this volume has had to be judiciously pruned. Leyland's tree alone could have stretched out roots and branches over most of the available space if their contributions in the early nineteen-twenties and with electric traction had not been curtailed. Likewise only a selection of the hosts of smaller British and foreign buses that flooded onto the British home market during this era is examined in any detail. Most of the remainder have been listed in two appendices.

It has not been possible to obtain colour transparencies of many of the vehicles described in the text since colour photography was not in general use. Hence it has been necessary to combine black-and-white photographs where possible (often of preserved vehicles) and to colour these by hand. We have also filled in the considerable gaps with artist's drawings based on black and white contemporary prints. I owe a debt of gratitude to Mr. Martin Rickitt for his help in supplying the coloured transparencies. In addition I am indebted to many others including Mr. J. Carroll, Mr. R. J. Gibson, Mr. C. Shears, the landlord of the Selsey Tram at Chichester, the general manager of Ashton-under-Lyne Transport Department and the staff of the British Museum Newspaper Library.

Grantham  
Spring 1970 David Kaye

A.D.C. = Associated Daimler Company
A.E.C. = Associated Equipment Company
B.A.T. = British Automobile Traction
B.H.&D. = Brighton, Hove & District
B.M.M.O. = Birmingham & Midland Motor Omnibus Company
B.R.C.W.C. = Birmingham Railway Carriage & Wagon Company
B.T.H. = British Thompson Houston
D.U.T. = Dublin United Tramways
E.C.O.C. = Eastern Counties Omnibus Company
E.C.W. = Eastern Coachworks
G.N.R. = Great Northern Railway
G.S.R. = Great Southern Railway
J.M.T. = Jersey Motor Transport
L.G.O.C. = London General Omnibus Company
L.N.E.R. = London North Eastern Railway
L.P.T.B. = London Passenger Transport Board
L.U.T. = London United Tramways
M.C.W. = Metro-Cammell Weymann
m.p.g. = miles per gallon
N.C.M.E. = Northern Counties Motor & Engineering
N.G.T. = Northern General Transport
P.M.T. = Potteries Motor Traction
P.R.V. = Park Royal Vehicles
p.s.v. = public service vehicle
r.p.m. = revolutions per minute
R.S.J. = Ransomes, Sims & Jefferies
S.M.C. = Sunbeam Motor Company
S.M.T. = Scottish Motor Traction
S.O.S. = Shire's Own Specification

N.B.—Throughout this work the *original* fleet numbers are used, although extensive renumbering has taken place in the case of many operators.

# INTRODUCTION

## 1. Reconstruction 1919

THE public road transport scene in 1919 was not very different from that before August 1914. In London the A.E.C. B class of 34-seater double-deckers reigned almost supreme and, like the B, other chassis being built in 1919 resembled the horse buses of the turn of the century. As yet no buses had been built with a purely motor omnibus design. The body was high off the ground, which necessitated the provision of a number of guard slats beneath the sides of the vehicles to prevent small children and dogs, from straying under the bus. This was the period when one chassis sufficed for bodies for double-deckers, single-deck buses and charabancs. Incidentally we seem to be returning to this state of affairs at the time of writing (1970), with the multi-purpose Daimler Fleetline in the van. Daimlers were busy in 1919 too, and had just added to their successful CC and CD range a more powerful CK chassis, which had a 22.4 h.p. engine (R.A.C. rating) that developed 30 b.h.p. at 1,000 r.p.m. Associated Equipment Company were building the Y and the YC chassis at their old Walthamstow factory and Tilling-Stevens at Maidstone were manufacturing their TT1 chassis. Leylands were producing their N series of chassis up in Lancashire, and at Basingstoke Thornycrofts were supplying operators with their J model. At Luton a limited number of Commer vehicles were coming off the assembly lines for the p.s.v. market. Compared with ten years later the choice open to operators was not very great, but then in most towns and cities in Britain the tramcar still ruled the roost. Indeed by 1919 most of the electric systems were less than twenty years old, although some of them were already showing wear and tear due to the neglect of maintenance during the Great War.

Writing in the *Commercial Motor* for 23 January 1919, the Editor, Edmund Dangerfield, stated: 'Now that "reconstruction" is the order of the day it is noteworthy to observe that most municipal tramway authorities propose meeting the demands for more travelling facilities by the provision of motorbuses.' He mentioned that Portsmouth were considering buying buses: 'because it is not possible to rely upon purchasing tramcars for months and months and months.' He added that

Barrow, Birkenhead, Lincoln, Liverpool, Sheffield, Tynemouth and Walthamstow were all feeling likewise. Nevertheless, it was not until 1929 that the first on this list (Lincoln) actually said goodbye to the last of its trams, and trams were still running in both Sheffield and Liverpool long after the end of the Second World War. At this date Birmingham Corporation owned a mere 52 motorbuses, whilst the total at Sheffield was a bare two dozen. Lancaster Corporation had turned to the small electric battery bus for a solution and were operating four of these, whilst York tried out another four. Six municipalities were using trolleybuses at the end of the First World War, but even Bradford ran only seventeen of these rather quaint looking vehicles and Leeds eight. Other places to use trolleybuses were Aberdare U.D.C., Keighley, Ramsbottom and Rotherham. In the first three years of peace there were only three new additions to their ranks, Tees-side (consisting of Middlesborough Corporation and Easton U.D.C.) on 8 November 1919; York (1920), and Halifax (20 July 1921). For most municipal operators the motorbus was needed for duties of feeder services for the tramway network, or for linking tramheads via sparsely populated routes.

In 1919 local authorities still had considerable powers in deciding what vehicles could traverse their streets, whether they owned these vehicles or not. The *Commercial Motor* pointed out in 1919 that London seemed to have tougher restrictions upon buses than other capital and major cities as regards both speed limits and weights (laden and unladen) and as the following table demonstrates:

|  | Speed Limit (m.p.h.) | Unladen Wt. (tons) | Laden Wt. (tons) |
|---|---|---|---|
| London | 12 | $3\frac{1}{2}$ | 6 |
| Paris | $13\frac{1}{2}$ | 5 | $7\frac{1}{2}$ |
| Berlin | $15\frac{1}{2}$ | $4\frac{1}{2}$ | $7\frac{1}{4}$ |
| New York | 20 | ? | 7 |

Consequently the total number of passengers per vehicle made operating in London less economical than in the other three cities. The average London double-decker sat 34, compared with 44 in New York and 45 in Berlin. Paris which had only single-deck buses, managed to exceed the London total with 35. Much research, therefore, went into the joint London General and A.E.C. K design, which combined the weight limits with a body capable of seating 46. Nevertheless, the *Commercial Motor* was not in favour of high capacity buses as the ensuing comment in the issue of 6 March 1919, shows: 'In our opinion, the number accommodated on the London tramcars namely 64, is too great, leading to non-collection of fares, lack of supervision at the entrance resulting in mishaps and delays to the whole service.'

It was suggested that perhaps 40 or 42 passengers might be the optimum number for a motorbus in London.

Some prophets were saying that the answer to the motorbus was to power it by a diesel engine, but in 1919 this was regarded as rather a doubtful starter since the weight of an equivalent diesel engined bus would be so much greater than that of the comparable petrol engined vehicle. At this date whereas a petrol engine could run at 1,000 r.p.m., a diesel unit rarely exceeded 450 r.p.m. and was thus too slow. This problem might be solved by equipping the petrol engine with more cylinders. Dangerfield, writing on 3 June 1919, favoured 6 cylinder units, for as he says: 'High power, with a 4 cylinder engine connotes cylinders of large diameter, and the process of swinging a 5 in. by 6 in. 4 cylinder engine is no light matter, even for the muscular.' He even suggested that 8 cylinder engines might be worth serious consideration. Although the 6 cylinder was to begin to win through before the end of that decade, it was not to be for another 50 years before the first 8 cylinder buses and coaches entered service.

Solids were still practically universal on commercial vehicles in 1919. An advertisement appearing in the *Commercial Motor* on 9 January 1919, on behalf of Wood-Milne solid band tyres, tells of a victory coach run on 1 December 1918, by a charabanc belonging to the North Wales Silver Motor Company of Llandudno, along an itinerary that included Conway, Bethesda, Nanffrancon Pass, Capel Curig, Bettws-y-Coed and Llanrwst. At the 1919 Olympia Show Dunlops demonstrated large 9 in. *pneumatic* tyres and Goodyear 8 in. tyres suitable for charabancs. It was not until the 1921 Commercial Motor Show at Olympia that Berliet, the French manufacturer, displayed a 30 h.p. coach chassis fitted with pneumatic tyres. At the same show Laffly showed their Laffly-Schneider Limousine Saloon Bus with pneumatic tyres supporting a 22-seat coach body. Even then it was thought to be a long time before the relatively heavy double-decker could be given this comfort.

However, a bumpy ride was not the only discomfort suffered by passengers riding on the 1919 double-decker bus. The *Commercial Motor* spoke up indignantly about an even more trying situation in the issue of 13 March 1919: 'No winter period goes by without the question of the feasibility of improving the London omnibus by covering in the upper deck being revived. This winter the need has been more urgently felt because of the removal of the knee aprons and because of the prevalence of influenza.

The objection of the police as licensing authorities to any proposals to this end has been the raising of the centre of gravity of the vehicle, but the existence of fair grounds for this objection has never been tested, and in any case, it can be met by underhanging the springs, so lowering the centre of gravity materially.'

There were, nevertheless, other problems to be overcome in this connection, such as those of low bridges, upper deck ventilation and interior lighting.

Every seaside resort had its line of charabancs plying for hire in 1919. The charabanc with its rows of seats, each with a separate door, was a reminder of the old horse-drawn era. Summer seasons in Britain are notoriously short. The small man has other jobs to turn to in the off-season, but the larger operator did not like to see his charabancs standing idle for half of each year. Attempts were being made at this time to convert the open ozone-blown pleasure vehicle into an all-the-year-round p.s.v. Early efforts were made by the London coach-building firm of Dodson Bros. with their so-called Charabus and Chelsea (the latter being fitted to a 30 cwt. Fiat chassis).

So far we have examined some of the problems facing the larger operators in 1919, but what of the small man?: 'The returning R.A.S.C. man who is considering the starting of a bus service will, therefore, have duly to consider the possibility of his being able to reckon on carrying on an average twenty people each journey, being able to collect 2d. per passenger for each mile run.' Grim, realistic advice indeed from the *Commercial Motor* to its readers on 27 March 1919. The small man could neither afford, nor required the typical models being put on the market by such manufacturers as Leylands. Their smallest bus chassis, the C1, weighed three tons and could seat 23. A new A.E.C. bus could be bought from their agents, United Automobile Services, for £1,000, but this price was well outside what a returning Royal Army Service Corps sergeant or major could afford. One solution was to buy a war surplus lorry or ambulance. This course was adopted by Mr. Walling of Eastergate, Sussex who started a service between Bognor and the village of Slindon in May 1919, using an ex-army Austin ambulance which he had converted into a 14-seater bus, entered from the rear. He then purchased another

Austin from the army, and this time he had it reconditioned by George Sherwood of Whetstone before having a new 20-seat Strachan & Brown body fitted to BP 8057. This enabled him to have the ambulance bodywork removed from BP 5007 and to have a proper 14-seat bus body mounted onto the chassis by Wadhams of Waterlooville, Hants.

For others the answer lay in the Model T Ford. Basically this could seat 14 passengers, but by adding an extension a further $3\frac{1}{2}$ ft. (or 6 passengers) could be gained. The most popular of these extension kits came from Baico, but others were supplied by Eros, Eto and Olsen.

The average small operator needed a very flexible vehicle, and so a removable bus body was of great merit in his eyes. With this in mind Leylands advertised B 8580 in 1919. This vehicle had a removable charabanc body, but was also pictured as a truck, filled with 'live sheep', or so the legend on the side led us to believe. When Mr. J. Mitchell, of Warnham, near Horsham, began operating about 1920 between that town and the villages of Colgate, Faygate and Rusper, he used his Ford T (BP 5973) as a coal lorry on occasions. On the other hand another small operator in the Horsham area, Mr. T. W. Carter, removed the roof from his Ford T and then took out all the seats. What remained of the bodywork then became a furniture van! Near York, Mr. Fentiman of Seaton Ross used the platform of his Ford T (BT 9420) as a market gardening lorry and transported produce to Selby market. Fortunately this vehicle is now being restored by youthful enthusiasts at the Lincoln Transport Museum. Another Ford T that now appears at rallies (BH 4081) was used by Wyatt of Yattendon, Bucks as a combined bus and village carrier. Garners of the Moseley Motor Works, Birmingham produced for the 1921 Show their 'Busvan' with its folding seats and unbreakable windows, and claimed that it was the 'complete utility' vehicle.

One interesting experiment was carried out in 1919, when Marconi's 'wireless telegraphy' was demonstrated on board National No. 190 (F 8040) between Chelmsford and Colchester. Passengers were able to listen to gramophone records being played at Broomfield, some ten miles off the route. A square aerial had been rigged up on the outside of the bodywork, near the platform, for this purpose.

## 2. *Away from the Old: 1920–9*

On 8 November 1919 the Tees-side trolleybus system was inaugurated, a system, which, although small, is still active in 1970, for not only was a further extension opened in 1968 but some of Reading's modern outcasts have also been added to the fleet. On 1 April 1968, the Tees-side board was absorbed under the Tees-side Transport Department, which also consisted of the erstwhile Middlesborough and Stockton-on-Tees bus fleets. The first ten trolleybuses were of Railless manufacture and were driven by 23 h.p. motors. The single-deck bodies seated 28. Soon other small networks were to evolve. York began their first attempt at a trolleybus operation in 1920, followed by Halifax on 20 July 1921. The next year Birmingham began operating their first route on 27 November, whilst London United Tramways carried out experiments with trolleybuses in the streets of Wimbledon, although it would be another decade before a regular service would run in the capital of tennis. 1923 was the year that saw one of the most famous of all the systems, Ipswich, commence. On 2 September, the first of a long line of home-town Ransomes, Sims & Jefferies' trolleys, took to the road. At the other side of England just over a month later (29 October) Wolverhampton also sampled the joys of locally built trolleybuses, this time of Guy manufacture. In 1924 it was the turn of West Hartlepool Corporation (28 February). The middle year of the nineteen-twenties was quite a boom year for trolleybus conquests: Wigan (7 May); Ashton-under-Lyne (26 August); Oldham (26 August) and Southend-on-Sea (16 October). In 1926 trolleybuses made their debut at Darlington (16 January) and Grimsby (2 October); the ensuing twelve months saw them running at Nottingham (10 April), Chesterfield (23 May) and St. Helens (11 July). The year 1928 started off with the opening of trolleybus routes in Hastings (4 January) and Maidstone (5 January). Doncaster followed suit later in the year (22 August).

On the other side of the account some trolleybus systems were already deemed to be failures during the nineteen-twenties and had been axed. Some were short lived indeed – such as Oldham's, which opted out of trolleybus operations just over a year after starting, on 5 September 1926. Halifax had lasted five years by the time the last trolley vehicle ran on 24 October 1926. York's first trial ended in 1929. Nevertheless, some earlier systems also 'bit the dust' during this decade as in the cases of Stockport (7 October 1919), Aberdare (1925) and Leeds (26 July 1928). The trolleybus of the nineteen-twenties, however, looked very much like the tramcar it was replacing, and we had to wait till the nineteen-thirties before it emerged into a shape in its own right, having passed through a distinct motorbus stage in between.

The commencement of trolleybus operation was not always the sign that the tramway system in that area was coming quickly to an end, for comparatively few came to the end of the line before 1930. Darlington (10 April 1926); Ipswich (26 July 1926); West Hartlepool (25 March 1927); Chesterfield (23 May 1927); Wolverhampton (1 December 1928); Mexborough and Swinton (10 March 1929) and Hastings (13 March 1929) could all be linked with trolleybus emergence, but elsewhere the cessation of tramcar operation was coupled with an expansion by motorbuses, and not always those belonging to the tramway operators either. There were three instances of this in the late nineteen-twenties. The tram routes of the City of Worcester were replaced after 31 May 1928, by motorbuses run by Midland Red, and those of the Burton and Ashby Light Railway had been treated in the same fashion as early as 1926. In this case Midland Red bought a new garage for its buses at Swadlincote to serve this new sphere of operations. Finally the red S.O.S. buses began to run over the old route linking Kidderminster and Stourport on 30 November 1928. Other tramway systems to disappear in this decade were those at Taunton (28 May 1921); Keighley (17 December 1924); Perth (19 January 1929); Lincoln (4 March 1929); Swindon (11 July 1929); Colchester (8 December 1929) and Burton-on-Trent (31 December 1929). Companies changed over to the motorbus working on the systems of Sunderland District Electric Tramways (12 July 1925), Potteries Electric Traction (11 July 1928) and Gosport & Fareham (31 December 1929). The Morecambe horse tramway, the last so operated in England, closed in 1924, and the Heysham Leyland petrol trams went in 1926. Jersey Eastern Railway was replaced by buses after 21 June 1929. The Douglas cable tramway ceased to operate on 19 August 1929.

The nineteen-twenties was par excellence the era of the foreign small bus in Britain. We have already mentioned the Model T Ford from the United States that became so popular with the ex-serviceman who had his eye on rural routes. The 1921 Olympia Show demonstrated that other American companies also had their eyes fixed firmly on our home market. Republic were offering two 14-seater coaches and a 20-seater bus, whilst Federal had both a coach and a bus version of their 20-seater on display. Wallace had 18- and 23-seater coaches for public view, whilst a strong challenge came from two French firms, Berliet with their 30-seater coach and de Dion Button with their 18- and 28-passenger coaches. From Italy came a 25-seat Lancia charabanc, along with a Fiat 14-seater coach and 13-seater bus. By the 1925 Show Chevrolet, Willys-Overland, Minerva and Reo had entered the p.s.v.

field in Britain, as had Renault, Latil, Gotfredson, Saurer and Fageol. Generally speaking the prices for these foreign chassis were cheaper than comparable ones from British manufacturers. For example, Frank Allen Ltd. of Brigg, Lincs. were offering to fit a 14-seat body (worth £165) to one-ton chassis of four continental and one British manufacture, and the overall price charged put the sole British firm (Morris) in fourth position, viz.:

| 1st | Ford | £272 |
| 2nd | Chevrolet | £314 |
| 3rd | Overland | £340 |
| 4th | Morris | £350 |
| 5th | Reo | £485 |

In the 20-seater range a Minerva at £540 compared very favourably with a solid tyres Daimler at £650 (with a further £100 to pay if pneumatics were fitted!).

The mid-'twenties were the days of the 'low-load-line'. There were the Maudslay Safety Low-level coaches and the Guy 'Low-load-line' bus and the Dennis 30 cwt. came, in places, within 10⅝ in. of the road surface. Steep steps were out, and so were wet laps on top decks. Nottingham Corporation in September 1925, placed into service on their Nottingham to Beeston route TO 1943, a Dennis 4-tonner with a roof over the top deck. However, a month later the Editor of the *Commercial Motor* still found it necessary to attack 'official callousness and lack of vision' for the fact that London was virtually outside the area of this improvement, although roofed double-deckers 'were in use in Lancashire many years ago traversing open, windswept country with no mishap of the kind to be recorded'. All this prompted Mr. G. Page of Southampton to design a rigid framed 78-seat double-decker (roofed in, of course) of overall length 29 ft. 6 ins. and with a central entrance positioned between the two 'rear' axles, these being 8 ft. 6 ins. apart. Although this remained a paper wonder, A.D.C. did construct a 104-seater bus (still a record for a British Isles motorbus), which ran as a works bus for the A.E.C. Southall (Middlesex) Works. The trouble with both of these vehicles was that the Ministry of Transport, as late as the autumn of 1927, was circularising local authorities suggesting that they should not license any bus over 26 ft. in length. At that time manufacturers were planning a series with a basic length 18 ins. longer than this. However, in October 1925 London General did place their first roofed-over double-deckers (NS 1734–7) into service, choosing route 100 from the Elephant and Castle to Epping Town.

However, double-deckers were not the only vehicles that got wet in an English 'Summer'. In November 1927, there was an interesting demonstration of a new quick folding hood for coaches and charabancs (although the latter were now slowly going out of fashion). With one man working a handle at the rear of a Tilling-Stevens B9A coach, the roof was folded back in 50 seconds flat. The designer was Thomas Tilling himself. Coaches were definitely improving, as an article in the *Commercial Motor* for 27 September 1927, underlined. Rural England Motor Coaches Ltd. had started an express service between Gloucester and London using a new Studebaker coach with a 20-seater Strachan & Brown body, fitted with curtains at the windows. Departing from Gloucester at 10 a.m., passengers should reach their destination in London at 3.30 p.m. at a single fare of 9/6d. (15/– return). Not that this venture was new, for on 7 May 1921, Midland Red inaugurated their first express route between Birmingham and Weston-super-Mare, following it up on 16 June with another service to Llandudno. In 1922 these successful routes were added to by others going to Aberystwyth and Blackpool. Nevertheless this was all very seasonable, so Southdown were really breaking fresh ground in the autumn of 1927, when they announced that in future three of their Brighton to London journeys would continue throughout the winter.

Another aspect of coaching was the pleasure tours. Advertising in 1925, the South Durham Motors Ltd. of Stockton-on-Tees stated that they were using 20-seater Karriers with pneumatic tyres for day excursions to Barnard Castle (60 miles; 6/–), York (98 miles; 8/6d.) and the Scarborough Circular (122 miles; 12/–). They were also operating three-day tours to Blackpool and six- or even seven-day extended tours of Scotland and Wales.

Other improvements in buses included disc clutches in place of cone clutches, 4 wheel brakes (some with servo-operated or servo-assisted mechanisms) and a general lightening of chassis weights. At the same time the power of engines was increasing far beyond those of 1919. For example a new 6 cylinder 4 wheel Guy chassis of the 1927 Olympia had an engine that developed as much as 80 b.h.p., whilst the 6 wheel version went as high as 100 b.h.p. No wonder the Public Omnibus Company of London had ordered some 62-seater buses on the latter chassis for their route 529 (Victoria to Winchmore Hill). Even the Bristol 4 cylinder GW engine could develop power up to 75 b.h.p.

Mention of the Public Omnibus Company reminds us that the nineteen-twenties were the era of cut-throat competition. In London the battle of the 'pirates' with the monolithic and long established London General began on 5 August 1922, when a certain Mr. A. G. Partridge drove his chocolate and primrose bus on route 11. Leylands had helped Partridge to finance this cock-a-snook at the A.E.C. stranglehold on the capital. Seventeen months later there were 500 'pirates' prowling the streets of London seeking passengers. As John Hibbs comments in his *The History of British Bus Services* (p. 89) : 'Furthermore, the pirates' buses were often superior to the General's. Their Dennises and Leylands were faster and many were operated by firms which aimed to rival the L.G.O.C. in technical improvement. Thus the introduction of covered tops, pneumatic tyres, 4 wheel brakes and other advances all owed their origin to the enterprise of independents.' William Allen started up his Premier Line with three Straker Squires built at Edmonton, with 46-seater open top Dodson bodies constructed at Willesden. No. 1 (XN 513), No. 2 (XM 9995) and No. 3 (XM 9888) roamed the streets in a way that is vividly recalled in Dryhurst's book *Premier, the Story of a London Pirate*: 'The plan of campaign in the early days of Premier followed fairly closely that of most other independents whose buses would skim whatever profitable trade offered itself anywhere. By this means high receipts per mile could be obtained at the expense, needless to say, of the General and its associates. The three Premiers could be found on as many as fourteen routes or sections of route in one day and could be found at points as far apart as Stanmore, Dulwich, Wanstead and Turnham Green.'

In 1921, B.A.T. had withdrawn its buses between Barrow-in-Furness and Ulverston. Within a short time no less than 60 owner-drivers were competing with 14-seaters. Eventually in 1927, 16 of these combined together to form a co-operative called the Furness Omnibus Company Ltd., which re-equipped the owner-drivers with new stock such as No. 1 (TD 6270), Leyland Leveret 20-seater and the large Leyland Lioness No. 12 (TD 9220). Between Littlehampton and Arundel in Sussex, 'pirates' such as West, used to leave the seaside resort a few minutes after the regular Southdown bus, chase it, overtake it, often driving recklessly, and arrive before the Duke of Norfolk's castle a couple of minutes ahead of the slower and larger Tilling-Stevens of the big operator.

The practice of Reo of giving eye-catching names to their models, Sprinter, Speed Wagon, Pullman and Major, began to find favour elsewhere by 1925. A small firm, Halley, called their trio Talisman, Ivanhoe and Kenilworth, after Sir Walter Scott's trilology. Now the giants stepped in, with A.E.C. using historic titles such as Renown, Blenheim, Ramillies and Grenville, and rivals Leylands chose the letter L for everything from the small Leveret up through the Lion, Lioness and Leopard, to the large Leviathan. Later, in 1927, Bean decided to call their 6 cylinder model Sir Galahad. By 1929 there was the Leyland Titan and the A.E.C. Regal, Regent and Ranger. Dennis Bros. got away from their alphabetical series after H had been reached and launched out into Arrow, Dart and Lance. The S.M.C. Sikh and Pathan, the Gilford Buda and Hera, the Crossley Alpha and Condor, the Albion Victor, Valkyrie and Valiant, and the Guy Wolf and Conquest, all followed in due time, but Daimlers kept on with their C series through CK and CL and CM, back to CG and CH, and on to CP and COG.

## 3. Order and Standardisation: 1930–9

What had seemed almost impossible to achieve in the improvement of motorbuses in 1919 – the covered top double-decker, pneumatics, 6 cylinder engines of infinitely greater power, low chassis frames, more seats – had become accomplished facts ten years later. Therefore as we move into the 'thirties, so we are entering an era of consolidation, rather than one of remarkable progress, although it was to this decade that one of those pipe dreams of 1919 came true, the diesel engined bus. By 1933, Guys were building only oil engined Arabs for the larger single-deck and all the double-deck market. By that date the A.E.C. 7·7 litre diesel engine was becoming an optional for both Regent and Regal, whilst close on their heels came that other giant, Leyland, with later versions of their Titan and Tiger. Gardners were beginning to break away from the tradition that an engine always had to have an even number of cylinders, by producing their 5LW unit. At the same time forward control had become the acceptable method of driving all but the smallest buses and the touring coaches. The six-wheeler phase was beginning to fade, expecially after 1935, except for large capacity double-deck trolleybuses.

Mention of trolleybuses reminds us that this decade witnessed the real triumph of that vehicle. With London Transport in the van, medium size fleets of these electric buses were quickly established, and systems such as Bradford's, which had seemed almost stagnant for a long time, began a new lease of life and growth, as new stock poured in from all quarters. In 1930, there were about 500 trolleybuses in the whole of Britain, whereas eight years later this had swelled to 3,000. Likewise mileage had gone up from 250 miles of route in 1932, to nearly 650 miles in 1938. A dozen trolleybus manufacturers were still active, some, such as Daimler, joining in for the first time. New systems appeared all over the U.K., viz.:

| | |
|---|---|
| 1930 | South Lancashire (1 August) |
| | Pontypridd (18 September) |
| 1931 | Walsall (22 July) |
| 1932 | Notts and Derby (7 January) |
| | Derby (9 January) |
| | Llanelly (26 December) |
| 1933 | Huddersfield (4 December) |
| | Bolton (17 December) |
| 1934 | Bournemouth (22 June) |
| | Portsmouth (4 August) |
| 1935 | Newcastle-upon-Tyne (1 October) |
| 1936 | Reading (18 July) |
| | South Shields (12 October) |
| 1937 | Cleethorpes (19 July) |
| | Kingston-upon-Hull (23 July) |
| 1938 | Manchester (1 March) |
| | Belfast (28 March) |
| 1939 | Brighton (1 April) |

As J. Joyce exclaims in his *Trolleybus Trails* (p. 107): 'Municipal delegations went to towns to inspect the shining new vehicles, and they returned full of enthusiasm to spread the gospel at home. The tram was now dead, they proclaimed, but phoenix-like it had been re-surrected in a new form.' Even so some trolleybus networks did fall by the wayside, though almost unnoticed amongst the new converts. York's second attempt at running a quartet of trolleys lasted only from 1931 until 5 January 1935. Ramsbottom U.D.C. (31 December 1930) and Keighley (31 August 1932) also closed down at this time. Although neither was extensive, the former had started as early as August 1913 and Keighley's system also dated from that pre-war year. Could only the new big networks really pay their way?

'The tram was now dead', this was a statement true of many towns and cities by 1939. Scrapyards were full of their mouldering carcases, people bought them to convert into caravans, hen coops, garage spare-part stores, and some escaped to other British networks or on board ships to the continent, to trundle on for many a long year. The following table of 'last runs' shows how widespread its demise was during the 'thirties:

1930   Chester (15 February)
      Dudley, Stourbridge & District Electric Traction Co. (1 March)
      Lancaster (31 March)
      Haslingden (1 May)
      Tyneside Tramways & Tramroads (Wallsend) (31 August)
      Yorkshire Traction (Barnsley) (31 August)
      Chatham (30 September)
      Peterborough Electric Traction Company (15 November)
      Cheltenham (31 December)

1931   Wigan (28 March)
      Lowestoft (8 May)
      Dundee, Broughty Ferry & District Tramway Company (15 May)
      Kirkcaldy (15 May)
      Exeter (19 August)
      Pontypridd (30 August)
      Tynemouth (31 August)
      Cork (30 September)
      Scarborough (30 September)
      Carlisle (21 November)
      Ayr (31 December)
      Stockton-on-Tees (31 December)
      Wemyss (31 January)
      Leamington & Warwick

1932   Accrington (31 March)
      Luton (31 March)
      Rawtenstall (31 March)
      Barrow-in-Furness (5 April)
      Wakefield (25 July)
      Rochdale (12 November)
      Dublin and Blessington (31 December)

1933   Gloucester (11 January)
      Llanelli (16 February)

1933   Walsall (30 September)
       Wallasey (30 November)
       Great Yarmouth (14 December)

1934   Torquay (31 January)
       Rhondda (1 February)
       Guernsey (9 June)
       Middlesbrough (9 June)
       Wakefield (31 October)
       Yorkshire Woollen District (Dewsbury, Batley & Birstall)
           (31 October)
       Northampton (15 December)
       Southport (31 December)

1935   York (5 January)
       Portsmouth & Horndean Light Railway Company
           (9 January)
       Aberdare (31 March)
       Derby (28 April)
       Burnley (8 May)
       Doncaster (8 June)
       Poole (8 June)
       Warrington (28 August)
       Norwich (10 December)
       Preston (15 December)

1936   St. Helens (1 April)
       Bournemouth (8 April)
       Falkirk (21 July)
       Nottingham (5 September)
       Portsmouth (10 November)
       Dover (31 December)

1937   Isle of Thanet (24 March)
       Lytham St. Anne's (24 March)
       Grimsby (31 March)
       Weston-super-Mare (11 April)
       Swansea (29 June)
       Dunfermline (5 July)
       Birkenhead (17 July)
       Cleethorpes (18 July)
       Newport, Mon. (5 September)

1938   Ashton-under-Lyne (1 March)

1939    Halifax (14 February)
          West Bromwich (1 April)
          Bath (6 May)
          Reading (21 May)
          Merthyr Tydfil (26 August)
          Brighton (31 August)

Not all corporation tramways were replaced by either municipally owned trolleybuses or motorbuses. For example Gloucester, Bath and Weston-super-Mare all came under Bristol Tramways and its subsidiary Bath Tramways. Dover's services were run by the East Kent Road Car Company, which also provided buses for the Isle of Thanet. Norwich and Peterborough, in future had Eastern Counties Omnibus Company running their local routes and Hants & Dorset Motor Services became responsible for local bus services at Poole.

Tramways were not the only form of rigid transport in the process of closing down just before the Second World War. Small branch lines were also passing from the scene. Near Brighton, in 1939, Southdown Motor Services started a new route 32 between Hove Station and the Devil's Dyke to replace the defunct train service between these two points. They had had to do the same for the Midhurst to Chichester service in West Sussex. After a disastrous fire at St. Aubin Station on the night of 18–19 October 1936, the Jersey Railway & Tramway was closed in favour of buses.

As the big four railway companies began the process of pruning their more unremunerative lines, so the motor express coach began to come into its own. There had been some bus stations built as early as the mid-'twenties, but it was the 'thirties that saw the first modern coach stations. Immediately, we think of Victoria Coach Station in the heart of London, which was opened in March, 1932. However, one of the most remarkable hubs of the British coach network is to be located in St. Margaret's Road in Cheltenham, where in 1932 on the premises of Black & White Motorways, Associated Motorways commenced their daily miracle of transferring thousands of passengers by day and night from one long distance coach to another and at the same time giving them all the creature comforts they needed to enable them to continue their journey happily. On a less grand scale was built the unusual combined bus and coach station in the Square at Bournemouth in 1930, which housed Hants & Dorset buses upstairs and Royal Blue coaches downstairs.

The name Associated Motorways reminds us that, partly due to the efforts of the 'powers-that-be' to reduce the enormous unemployed force in Britain in the early 'thirties, a programme of road building and reconstruction, not seen since the turnpike era of two centuries before, was begun. Concrete dual carriageways and by-passes sprang up, starting with the famous Kingston by-pass along which was diverted the busy Portsmouth traffic on the A 3. If only September 1939 had not cut this programme short! Express coaches and long distant buses now had the surfaces and space they needed to show their true paces.

More sedate were the needs of the holidaymakers. Those who were lucky enough to have full-time work began to be given a week's paid holiday each summer. For them new types of buses were needed. Southdown retained their twenty-three open top Titan TD1s, along with an equally outdated Tilling-Stevens B10A2, to take these folk from Brighton to the Devil's Dyke on route 27, or along the coastal A 259 road to Worthing on route 31F. Other double-deckers were fitted with folding canvas roofs, inappropriately called 'sunshine roofs'. And the Bedford WTB took them out to mock-medieval cottages for strawberry teas at inflated prices.

Yes, we now think of the Bedford as native to Britain, but whereas most of the foreign owned chassis builders, like Lancia, Reo, Latil and Renault were not selling many of their wares on the British market, the American owned parent company, Vauxhalls, as from 1931, had been capturing large sections of the small coach demand, so by 1939 no less than 70 per cent. of all small buses and coaches coming into service in the United Kingdom were of Bedford manufacture. Of the other foreign owned firms, only Dodge and Opel seemed to be precariously surviving this onslaught by one of the grandchildren of General Motors.

However, not only were overseas manufacturers feeling the pinch, but some famous and long established British names were also passing into oblivion. Sunbeam had bought out Karriers, and apart from trade nameplates on certain trolleybuses, they had virtually disappeared from the p.s.v. market. Thornycroft and Tilling-Stevens, once giants in the motorbus industry, were now almost dwarfs, and soon after the Second World War was over they too could only be mourned. Straker-Squire, Railless, Gilford, Bean and others were no longer to be found on the stands of the Commercial Motor Show as the 'thirties drew to a close.

The collossus of the decade was undoubtedly the 1930 Road Traffic Act. Before Parliament in its wisdom decided to bring *the law* into the motor age, regulations governing the running of bus services were found in such antiquated legislation as the Stage Carriage Act of 1832 and the Town Police Clauses Acts of 1847 and 1889. As John Hibbs states in his *The History of British Bus Services* (p. 108): 'They applied only to vehicles plying for hire on the streets and so omitted most express coach operation, which used private land for terminal purposes. In addition, the Town Police Clauses Acts were permissive and by no means all the local authorities which were supposed to administer them had adopted the powers they gave. Others interpreted them in a number of different ways. Finally since they were intended for the licensing of horse-drawn vehicles, they applied only within local authority boundaries, so that a service running through industrial Lancashire required buses licensed by each authority through whose area they passed. In most country districts there was no licensing at all. Through the new Act, England and Wales were now divided into ten 'traffic areas', whilst Scotland was made one whole area on its own. The traffic commissioners were responsible for issuing certificates of fitness for the actual vehicles as well as licensing the actual services run. This spelt the end for unscrupulous 'pirates' with their cut prices, erratic and dangerous schedules and often poorly maintained vehicles. It enabled the large operators to grow larger, and the nineteen-thirties was the time when they swallowed up many of the smaller fry of their competitors.

Medium-sized independents like Lancashire United and Bartons became rare. The bulk of the routes were in the hands of members of large groups. Hence in southern England British Electric Traction was comprised of Aldershot & District, East Kent, Maidstone & District, Southdown, Devon General, City of Oxford; the Red & White group owned Red & White, Cheltenham & District, South Midland Motor Services (of Oxford), Venture (of Basingstoke) and Newbury & District; the Tillings group consisted of Bristol Tramways, Bath Tramways, Western National, Southern National, Wilts & Dorset, Hants & Dorset, Southern Vectis, Brighton, Hove & District, Eastern National, Eastern Counties and United Counties. In Scotland nearly all the bus operators were members of S.M.T. (e.g. Western S.M.T., Alexanders, Highland Omnibuses etc.), leaving David MacBrayne as the largest independent. In Ulster the Northern Ireland Road Transport Board was set up, which ran practically all bus routes not in the hands of either Belfast Corporation or the Great Northern Railway. Eire was, of course, not affected by the 1930 Act, but even here most of the services became concentrated in the hands of either Dublin United Tramways or the Irish Omnibus Company (whose bus routes and vehicles were transferred to the Great Southern Railway as from the beginning of 1934).

Perhaps the greatest piece of rationalization of all was the establishment of the London Passenger Transport Board on 1 July 1933, which took over control of all local bus services, Green Line express coach routes, underground trains, trams and trolleybuses, not only in the Central London area, but also in what were then largely rural districts on the periphery of London in Kent, Sussex, Surrey, Berkshire, Buckinghamshire, Bedfordshire, Hertfordshire and Essex. This included services run by such companies as Maidstone & District and Thames Valley. Hosts of small firms were acquired by the new board outside London itself, e.g. Amersham & District and the Penn Bus Company, both working in the Chilterns. Into the largely standardised fleets of the L.G.O.C., Thomas Tilling, Public, etc. came a flock of small vehicles such as Beans, Reos, Lancias, Gilfords, etc. Most of these were either sold straight away by the L.P.T.B., or else soon replaced by their own new standardised orders.

Bell Punch tickets were almost universal in 1930 and some, such as those used in London suburbs and by Bournemouth Corporation, had grown very long as routes were extended and more and more stages added to the tickets. By the middle of the decade experiments were beginning on machines like the T.I.M. that could print the relevant information such as fare, stage boarded, route, date, company's name and regulations.

The 'twenties had been the time when destinations were shown on a series of boards, fore, aft and to port and starboard, but from the 1929 series of new models, this information gradually began to appear on roller blinds in all four places. Normally these were printed white on black, but sometimes as in the case of the 'via' blinds on Bournemouth Corporation double-deckers, the different streets came in a variety of colours so that would-be passengers could spot immediately whether the trolleybus was for instance going along Old Christchurch Road (blue blind) or Bath Road (red blind). West Bridgford U.D.C. seemed to feel that their clients were rather short-sighted, since the route number figures were painted 2 ft. high and usually just one name, the terminus, was displayed in huge capital letters. Most operators who used symbols to show which route a bus was on, chose numbers, but Portsmouth Corporation used letters for their motorbus routes and numbers for their trolleybus routes. Furthermore a different number or letter was used for each direction (e.g. 3: Cosham – Southsea; 4: Southsea – Cosham).

## 4. Wartime Retrenchment: 1939–45

When the sirens sounded over much of southern Britain on the morning of Sunday, 3 September 1939, there were none of the scenes of joyful anticipation such as had occurred on 4 August 1914, for this time much of the population of Britain knew what total war meant. The damage that had been suffered during the Kaiser's War by Zeppelins and battleships would surely be trebled by the Dorniers, Junkers and Heinkels taking part in Hitler's War? Hence precautions had to be taken at once. All cream or light coloured bus roofs were painted darker to prevent them being conspicuous to enemy aircraft. All lights, both internal and external, on vehicles had to be drastically shaded. This resulted in more time being allowed after dark to complete a journey, which often meant buses departing at irregular intervals on routes that for years had known a constant frequency from crack of dawn until late at night. Last departures from towns were made an hour or more earlier, and indeed many evening journeys were axed from the time-table altogether, since with frequent night raids few ventured from their own homes. Sunday morning services were nearly all abandoned since most routes commenced only about 1 p.m. that day.

Never since the days of the Norman Conquest had our lives been so regulated. From 1941, six or more people waiting at a bus stop had to form an orderly queue. This at least prevented the wild rushes for crowded buses that was such an undignified feature of pre-war Britain. Mind you, due to fuel shortages, many bus stops were either amalgamated or else disappeared altogether so that less petrol or oil was wasted with the engine uneconomically ticking over. As the U boats sank more and more of our tankers so the fuel available for public transport grew less. Routes had to be curtailed, amalgamated or even abandoned completely. In Jersey under the German occupation, things grew so bad that one of the ex-Tram-O-Car Shelvoke & Drewry Freighters had its body removed by J.M.T. and this was then mounted on a trolley, and drawn by horse round the streets of St. Helier. On the mainland many operators tried out various kinds of gas producing trailers to be towed behind a bus. London Transport adapted some 170 of their ST class for this purpose.

Fuel was not the only thing in short supply. Staff too were scarce. Conductors became drivers as their mates (often fitter physically than them) were called up to the forces. Women took the conductors' places, and in a few cases the drivers' too. With maintenance staff also joining the Armed Services this resulted in buses being run with the minimum of care, particularly in the case of their bodywork.

Some operators did not need all their fleet; others had extra troops or airmen to move. East Kent were in the former category, as were Bournemouth. Hence five East Kent TD5s were sent to Southdown in 1940, who painted them in their own livery (although they were only on loan) and changed the previous numbers AJG 31–5, to 301–5. In November of that year they went further west to Devon General, who repainted them as Nos. DL 301–5. In 1943 they returned home to Kent. Bournemouth Corporation lent trolley buses to several systems between December 1940 and August 1945. Nos. 78/9 (AEL 406/7) had quite an adventurous time, for they first went to the L.P.T.B. (1940–2), then on to Newcastle-upon-Tyne (1942–3), thence to South Shields (1943), and finally to Walsall (1943–5). Nos. 77 (AEL 405) and 123 (ALJ 997) visited Llanelly during the period 1943–5. Twelve other Bournemouth trolleys spent the war at Wolverhampton. On the other hand, from July 1942 to the first half of 1943, Bournemouth itself had to borrow six of London Transport's ST class (Nos. 839, 979, 984, 985, 1001 and 1025). Whilst Blandford Camp was being constructed just before the war no less than 119 buses were required each day by Wilts & Dorset to transport the building workers! The Salisbury-based company thus set about buying up second-hand buses for such huge undertakings. They purchased forty-one Titan TD1s from Southdown alone, as well as a further sixteen of this type from neighbouring Hants & Dorset. Other TD1s came from Maidstone & District (3), Chatham & District (4), Bolton Corporation (4), Ribble (8), Tyneside Tramways and Tramroads (4) and Birkenhead Corporation (6). In addition Regents were acquired from Brighton, Hove & District (3), Nottingham Corporation (4) and Huddersfield Corporation (2).

The War Department had called up many buses and coaches for troop transport at the beginning of the war. For example Thames Valley lost Nos 158/61 (RX 1397/6), a pair of Tilling-Stevens B9As, and Nos. 240/1 (RX 9308/9) two Leyland Tiger TS4s, in this way. None of the four was ever returned to the company.

To make up for this shortage of vehicles several measures were taken. Old chassis, due to be scrapped as obsolete, received new engines or new bodywork, or both. The Ministry of Supply released a number of chassis during 1941–2, that had been 'frozen' since Dunkirk. These included 92 A.E.C. Regents, 85 Bristol K5Gs, 196 Leyland Titan TD7s, 15 Bristol L5Gs, 25 Dennis Lancet IIs, 22 Leyland Tiger TS11s, and 12 Tilling-Stevens H5LA4s. The recipients varied from L.P.T.B. with STL 2648–81 (Regents), B1–9 (K5Gs) and STD 101–11 (TD7s), and Midland Red with Nos. 2432–40 (TD7s) and 2441–6 (Regents). down to really small operators like King Alfred, Winchester (TD7: ECG 639) and Simpson, Rosehearty (H5LA4: BSA 367).

From late 1942 a trickle of new chassis began to appear: the Guy Arab I, the Daimler CWG5, the Karrier W4, the Bedford OWB. All bodywork had to comply with strict utility regulations in order to save as much valuable raw material for the war effort as possible. Some operators used ingenuity and Mansfield & District put onto the road in 1942, a pair of Commer Superpoise tractors, pulling trailer buses seating 38 passengers and numbered 27/8 (FVO 762/3) in their fleet.

During the so-called 'phoney war' of the autumn in 1939, yet two more tramway systems closed. On 1 October the last trams ran in Dudley, Oldbury, Rowley Regis, Smethwick and Tipton. Due to naval requirements the Douglas Head Marine Drive tramway to Port Soderick closed down on 15 September 1939. Bristol's trams ceased to run after 11 April 1941 and those of Southend-on-Sea came to an end on 8 April 1942. However, perhaps the most dramatic event in this field was the finish of the Coventry network during the night of 14 November 1940, when much of the centre of the city (including the cathedral) was reduced to ashes and twisted girders after the famous fire bomb raid by the Luftwaffe. The only new trolleybus system started during the war was in Cardiff, where it began on 1 March (St. David's Day!) 1942, with a small fleet of A.E.C. 664Ts. Talking of trolleybuses, London Transport added to their fleet by taking delivery of three batches of vehicles originally destined for Durban or Johannesburg, South Africa. Eighteen A.E.C. 664Ts, each with an 8 ft. wide M.C.W. bodywork (Nos. 1747–64, GLB 747, etc.), had English Electric 408 motors, Leyland TB7s were divided between Nos. 1722–33 (GGW 722/GLB 723, etc.) with M.C.W. 72-seat bodies and G.E.C. WT266C motors and Nos. 1734–46 (GLB 734, etc.) with the same bodywork, but with Metro-Vick 206D1 motors. All these trolleybuses of the SA1,

SA2 and SA3 classes were stationed at Ilford Depot. Special permission had to be sought since the legal width of buses in Britain at that date was 7 ft. 6 ins.

Before V.J. Day in August 1945 some measure of normality had already begun to return to the British transport scene. Buses and trolleybuses were beginning to be repainted in their old liveries in many towns, the hard wooden seats in the Bedford OWBs and Guy Arabs were in some cases being given a kind of upholstery, certain coach firms were even running short local excursions, and those buses that had pulled gas producing trailers had been converted back to normal petrol or diesel operation. A start had also been made to rebodying or rebuilding many venerable buses and coaches, so that they could fill the gaps in the post-war fleets until sufficient new stocks became available. Indeed, the British bus industry was on the threshold of its greatest boom, which reached its zenith in 1949.

1    LS 3 (UC 2201) was one of London General's famous 'London Sixes' based on the **A.D.C. 802** chassis.

2    Bull motors powered Bradford Corporation's No. 543 (KW 203), a 1927 vintage **A.D.C. 603** trolleybus with a Strachan & Brown body.

3   One of the most popular double-deck chassis types of the early 1920s was the **A.E.C. Y.** Here we see one as East Surrey's No. 20 (PA 9575).

4   Kingston-upon-Hull Corporation's (AT 2934) was a single-deck version of the **A.E.C. K.**

5 'En route' for Waltham Cross is London Transport's **S424**.

6 TY6470 was an **A.E.C. Reliance** employed on the express route between Glasgow and London.

7   Originally RT 97, FXT 272 was modified as a double-
    deck Green Line coach and renumbered RTC 1. It
    was an **A.E.C. Regent.**

8   No. 1 in the fleet of Elite was UR 7002, an example
    of an **A.J.S. Pilot.**

9 BMG 703 was an **Albion Victor PK115** with a 26-seat Duple body. It started life with F. H. Crook of Booker, Bucks, before becoming Thames Valley No. 349.

10 Owens ran this **Bean** (RX 7554) on their Windsor-Farnham Royal service.

11 Rayners of Horsham operated this second-hand **Berliet** (DO 3633) on a town route. Note the platform doors.

12 United Automobile's BJ 154 (AHN 406) was a **Bristol JO5G.**

13   Silver Queen of Eastergate, Sussex, ran RV 290, a
     normal control **Commer**.

14   Looking more like a car than a bus was ME 6966, an
     L.G.O.C. **Crossley**.

15 VU 7404 was a **Crossley Condor** with a Strachan body, No. 34 in the fleet of Manchester Corporation.

16 RJ 3014 started life as Salford Corporation's No. 115. It was a **Crossley Mancunian** with a 48-seat Metro-Cammell body.

17  'The Southsea Queen' was a **Dennis 3-tonner** in the ranks of the Southsea Tourist Company.

18  Aldershot & District operated this **Dennis H** (OU 1112) on a local route at Guildford.

19 Bourne & Balmer of Croydon owned this **Dennis Arrow** as their No. 25 (OY 3291).

20 This **Dennis Lance** had just passed from Red Rover into L.P.T.B. hands, as their DL 28, when this view was taken.

21 A 32-seat Beadle body was fitted to this **Dennis Lancet**, which was No. 3319 (EV 6054) in the fleet of Eastern National.

22 KX 6551 was a small **Dodge** bus used by Owens in Windsor.

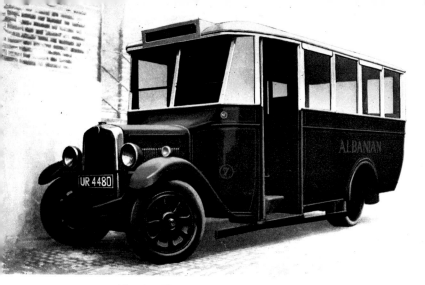

23  Albanian No. 7 (UR 4480) was a product of the
American **G.M.C.**

24  F. H. Kilner of Loxwood used this **G.M.C.** (CN 4097)
with its 24-seat body on his Horsham-Plaistow route.

25 Popular in the 1920s were **Guy Runabouts** such as Southern National 2857, employed as a toastrack tourist attraction at Bridport.

26 Leicester Corporation's No. 15 (RY 4373), **Guy B** with a Brush 25-seat body, started off the new Welford Place–Knighton Lane, one-man-operated route, in 1927.

27　Derby Corporation's No. 26 (CH 8836) was a **Guy BTX.**

28　South Lancs. Nos. 45 (TJ 3334) and 37 (TJ 3326) stand idle at the end of their working life. They were **Guy BTX** trolleybuses with 48-seat Roe bodywork.

29    A typical **Karrier** single-decker of 1930 vintage is
Allitt & Sons' bus on London route 202.

30    This vehicle acted as a **Karrier WL6** demonstrator.

31  Lewis of Watford owned this **Lancia** (MT 3017) with
its two doors and period canvas roof.

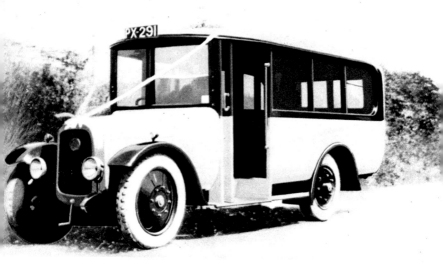

32  Mr. Walling, the proprietor of Silver Queen of Eastergate, used one of his pair of **Latil** buses (PX 291) to
carry guests to his wedding.

33 Solid tyres, wooden spokes and five life guard slats
help to date Empire Best's **Leyland N** (MH 2484).

34 London Transport's TC2 was a **Leyland Titanic
TT1,** used on route 18.

35  **Leyland Cheetah LX3** (EUF 500) with its 24-seat central entrance Park Royal coach body is seen here by Southdown's Beachland Bus Station on Hayling Island.

36  EV 3403 was a **Maudslay ML** which started with Gordon, before it became MY 1 in General's fleet.

37    Red Rover of Feltham ran this 16-seat Maxwell (BP 9579) on their Bognor-Middleton route.

38    Imperial No. 11 (VX 9932) was a **Morris-Commercial Dictator** used on the Rainham run.

39  Swiss built **Saurers** were found with some small
operators during the late 1920s. Such was the case with
RD 9751 of Comfy Cars.

40  Originally with Price of Dinas Powis, TX 1506, a
**Shelvoke & Drewry Freighter,** was bought by
Abbotts of Exmouth. Note its tiny wheels.

41    W. Gates of Worthing used the **Shelvoke & Drewry Freighters** on his Tram-O-Car routes. No. 11 (PO 9665) had a 26-seat Harrington body.

42    Crosville used **Shelvoke & Drewry Freighters** with toastrack seating at Rhyl and Barmouth. Their U13 (CFM 341) had an Eastern Coachworks body.

43 For a short while RO 8852 was one of the few **Star Flyers** in the ranks of London Transport.

44 Isle of Man Road Services No. 54 (MN 5943) is an example of a **Thornycroft**.

45 A later **Thornycroft** is seen here. JH 1587 started with Peoples, before it was acquired by the L.P.T.B.

46 Thomas Tilling used XN 7329, a 1923 vintage **Tilling-Stevens TS3** petrol-electric, on their route 1 C.

47 East Surrey used **Tilling-Stevens Express B10A**s
such as PK 4244 with its Short Bros. all-metal body of
1928 vintage.

40    Prior to entering the Canvey fleet as No. 15, UF 3589
      had been a Southdown **Tilling-Stevens B10A2** with
      a 32-seat Tilling body.

49    A solid-tyred **Vulcan** was DY 2027, the West Hill Bus
      of Bexhill-on-Sea.

50 Dowles of Singleton, Sussex, operated this **Vulcan VSD** (BP 8429) of 1922.

51 Rayners of Horsham employed this **W & G Du Cros** charabanc (KK 4403) for outings.

52  Not much is known about this **A.D.C. 423** of South
Yorkshire, which is to be restored by the Lincolnshire
Vintage Vehicle Society.

53   At the 1968 Brighton Rally stands **S742**, a former
L.G.O.C. 54-seater **A.E.C.** recently restored by Charles
Banfield.

54    London General's **K424** was an **A.E.C.** product of
1920, seen here 'en route' for Brighton.

55    Housed at the British Transport Museum at Clapham
is this **A.E.C. NS** type (1955, YR 3844) of 1927 vintage.

56 Being repannelled by her new owners at Crawley is former London General T31 (UU 6646), a 1929 **A.E.C. Regal I.**

57 Another **A.E.C. Regal** is FV 4548, a former Ribble bus, which ended her days as a mobile classroom for learner drivers.

58 Near the Hoeford depot of the Fareham & Gosport Omnibus Company is one of their long lived **A.E.C. Regent I**s.

59 Another **A.E.C. Regent I** was RD 7127, here seen as a works bus for Linfields, growers of Thakeham, Sussex, in September 1962.

60 In May 1965 the above bus looked quite different, having been restored to its Reading Corporation livery (No. 47) by the Reading Transport Society.

61 A preserved **A.E.C. Regent** of London Transport is their STL 1871 (DLU 240).

62   A later **A.E.C. Regent** of London Transport, which has also been saved from the scrapyard is RT 44 (FXT 219) of 1933 vintage.

63   Brighton Corporation's No. 67 (FUF 67) is another **A.E.C. Regent** of that year. Here it is at Hove Station in July 1962.

64 Standing at their Chilwell headquarters is Barton's No. 618 (FNW 722), a Roe-bodied **A.E.C. Regent** which started life as Leeds Corporation's 722.

65 In process of being restored by the R.T.S. is **A.E.C. 661T** (ARD 676), which was No. 113 in the Reading Corporation fleet.

66    Brighton Corporation's **A.E.C. 661T** No. 32 (FUF 32)
lies quietly awaiting the end at Light's Yard at Lewes
in October 1963.

67    London General's **A.E.C. Renown** of 1931 vintage,
LT 165 (GK 5323) has been preserved by the British
Transport Museum at Clapham.

68  Making a comback on the last day of trolleybus operation in the London area is the original 'Diddler'
L.U.T.'s No. 1 (HX 2756), an **A.E.C. 663T.**

69  Being towed to Brighton during the 1966 London-
Brighton run is former London Transport **A.E.C.
664T** No. 260 (CUL 260).

70  Crossing Castle Junction in 1963 is Belfast Corporation's **A.E.C. 664T** No. 92 (FZ 7877). It has a typical
68-seat Harkness body.

71  One of Cardiff Corporation's first trolleybuses was
**A.E.C. 664T** No. 207 (CKG 197) with its 70-seat
Northern Counties body.

72    A rear view of another of this group (No. 201, CKG 191).
Note the large bumpers at the rear.

73    An example of an **A.E.C.-M.C.W. chassisless** trolleybus is London Transport's No. 1449 (FXH 449).

74  Like the above trolleybus, 1521 (FXH 521) also had a
70-seat M.C.W. body. It has been preserved for
posterity.

75  A 1963 Brighton Rally bird's eye view of **A.E.C. Q**
CGJ 174, which once was Q69 in the L.P.T.B. fleet.

76 Another view of Q69 showing the position of the side
engine fitted against its Birmingham Railway Carriage
Works body.

77 This small Austin bus was once No. 2854 in the
Southern/Western National fleet.

78    Formerly No. F55 in the Alexander fleet is WG 1448,
an example of the **Albion Valkyrie PW 65** of 1932.

79    Although built after 1945 South Yorkshire's GWT 630,
is a typical **Albion Venturer.**

80 **Albion SPLB41** (US 6798) spent most of its life with a Glasgow convent.

81 Taking part in the H.C.V.C. Rally in May 1962 is AAA 756, an **Albion Victor PHB49** and TM 9347, the first **Bedford** coach ever built.

82 A 1935 vintage **Bedford WLB** is CMG 30, seen here outside Worthing Town Hall during a local Rally.

83 In 1939 FEL 216 and FEL 218 were new **Bedford WTB** buses with Bournemouth Corporation, but today they are cherished by Poole Model Railway Society.

84 South Notts. Bus Company owned this **Bedford OWB,** seen here at their Gotham headquarters.

85 Note the wartime 'utility' appearance of the bodywork of this **Bedford OWB,** ending its working life with a contractor.

86 Guildford, July 1962, and preserved BWT 794, a
**Bristol JO5G** of 1937 that was once in the West
Yorkshire Road Car fleet.

87 One of the longest serving **Bristol K5G**s was CDL 899,
which used to be No. 702 in the fleet of Southern Vectis,
who used it on their summer routes based on Shanklin.

88 At its Boundary Road, Hove terminus is Brighton, Hove & District's No. 995 (FHT 112), a **Bristol K5G,** which came from Bristol Tramways.

89 The wartime shape of the Duple body on Colchester Corporation's **Bristol K6A** No. 46 (KEV 331) looked rather out-of-place by 1963.

90    North Western Road Car were a non-Tilling user of
the **Bristol L5G,** one of which, No. 364 (AJA 118),
has been preserved for us.

91    Immaculately restored to its former glory is this
Bush & Twiddy-bodied **Chevrolet LQ** (VF 8157) of
1931.

92   PO 966 was a **Chevrolet** which was used by its Stor-
rington (Sussex) owner for both goods and passengers.

93   Waveney-bodied JC 4557 was a **Commer PN3** in the
fleet of Llandudno U.D.C.

94  At most rallies will be found ex-Birmingham Corporation No. 1107 (CVP 207), a **Daimler COG5** with an
M.C.W. body.

95　A **Daimler COG5-40** single-decker is GNU 750 preserved after its withdrawal from the fleet of Tailby & George of Willington.

96　West Bridgford U.D.C. bought this **Daimler CWA6** for their No. 27 (CCX 779) from Huddersfield Corporation in 1955.

97 Belfast Corporation No. 484 (GYL 290) is a **Daimler CWA6** which, after serving with London Transport as their D 125, was given a new Harkness body by its new owners.

98 Douglas Corporation No. 51 (FMN 954) was a **Daimler CWA6** with a Duple body.

99   West Bromwich Corporation bought No. 32 (EA 4181) in 1929. This **Dennis E** has a Dixon body, and now appears frequently at rallies.

100   Glenton Tours of London now run this 1929 vintage **Dennis GL** toastrack (CC 9305), which ran up the Great Orme for Llandudno U.D.C. in its early days.

101    Twin to the last vehicle is another Roberts toastrack Llandudno **Dennis GL.** CC 8694 is owned by Southampton University Engineering Society. Beside it stands **Dennis Mace** CYF 163.

102    Sparshatts have lavished loving care on this restored **Dennis 30 cwt.** bus.

103 Dennis Bros. of Guildford own this **Dennis Dart,** which originally worked at Morecambe.

104 At Grayshott in May 1963 was **Dennis Ace** ECV 412 with its Plymouth-built Mumford body.

105   'Polly' has been rescued from a scrapyard fate. She is a 1939 **Dennis Falcon,** that started life as No. 81 (FUF 181) in the fleet of Southdown.

106   BH 4081 is a 1920 **Ford Model T** with a **Baico** extension, belonging to Wyatt of Yattendon, Bucks.

107 This **Garford** lorry chassis is identical to that used for
their buses in the mid-1920s.

108 Mulleys keep DX 9547 in good trim. It is a **Gilford**
**AS6** of 1931 with an Eaton body.

109    Appearing at Sheffield Park of Bluebell Railway fame in 1964 is this famous **Gilford 168OT,** GW 713.

110    With a utility style low bridge Strachans body is Barton's 449 (GNN 710), a **Guy Arab II.**

111   Another **Guy Arab** with a similar Weymann body is
Highland Omnibuses No. E39 (EFS 356) at Inverness
in 1962.

112   Walsall No. 7 (JDH 268) with its highbridge Park
Royal body was a **Guy Arab II,** here seen on learner
duties.

113    In 1963 Southdown's **Guy Arab II** No. 439 (GUF 139) was operating summer route 102 to Devil's Dyke. It had a Northern Counties body, which had been converted to open top.

114    An East Lancs. body was fitted to Aldershot & District No. 890 (EOR 27), seen at Guildford in 1965. Another **Guy Arab II.**

115    Ashton-under-Lyne Corporation's No. 70 (FTE 889) is an example of a **Guy Arab** with a Crossley body new in 1952.

116    London Transport's G351 (HGC 130) is a **Guy Arab** with a Park Royal body has been preserved for us.

117  Ending its days as a 'building' at Nutbourne, Sussex, is a **Guy BT** trolleybus that was once in Hastings Tramways fleet.

118  Standing beside 'Happy Harold', the famous open-top **Guy BTX** trolleybus No. 3A (DY 4695), is Hastings Tramways No. 32 (BDY 807), a post-war **Sunbeam 'W'**.

119     Taking part in a rally at Worthing is Southdown's 813
(UF 4813), a **Leyland Titan TD1,** 1929 Brush-bodied
vehicle.

120     Restored at Clapham as Eastern Counties No. A001,
in actual fact **Leyland Titan TD1,** DR 4902 was
Southern National 2849.

121   Wallace Arnold's JUB 29 is a marriage of a Glasgow **Leyland Titan TD1** chassis with a West Yorkshire body.

122   Proceeding along the Crawley by-pass on a Brighton Rally is J.M.T. No. 25 (J 6332) an all-**Leyland Titan TD2**.

123 **Leyland Titan TD3** AUF670 was Southdown No. 970 and had a new East Lancs. body before it entered service with Dengates of Beckley, Sussex.

124 A striking frontal shot of a sister vehicle at Clarence Pier, Southsea, is No. 7 (RV6367) in its newer role as a summer tourist attraction.

UNICORN GATE

129

RV 6370

125 All-**Leyland Titan TD4** (RV 6370) was Portsmouth
Corporation No. 129 when it was caught here on a
Docks service.

126　Passing Prince's Park is Eastbourne Corporation's 1936 vintage No. 96 (JK 5606), another all-**Leyland Titan TD4.**

127　Ex-Southdown **Leyland Titan TD5** (EUF 196) had its Beadle body rebuilt before it was sold to Hutfields of Gosport.

128    Converted into a canteen at Lower Mosley Street, Manchester, is ex-Rochdale Corporation No. (DDK 117), a N.C.M.E.-bodied **Leyland Titan TD5.**

129    Formerly in the fleet of Wigan Corporation JP 4712 is a **Leyland Titan TD7** with a low bridge Leyland body.

130    At the Horsham Rally in 1964 are Southdown 228 (FUF 228), a **Leyland Titan TD5** (since broken up) and Southdown 4 (CUF 404), a Harrington-bodied **Leyland Cub KPZ.**

131    AFR 900 was a **Leyland Cub** with a luxurious Burlingham coach body, and was used by Committees of Blackpool Corporation.

132 Saved for preservation at Bolney, Sussex, stands CLE 122, a **Leyland Cub KP2,** originally C96 in London Transport's fleet.

133 One of the earliest **Leyland Lion PLSC1**s was 1927 vintage KW 474 of Blythe & Berwick, now restored in Lincoln Corporation livery.

134   Used as a showman's caravan, but now 'rescued', is
ex-Hants & Dorset Corporation **Leyland Lion PLSC3**
RU 8678.

135   Having spent some years in Jersey, BR 7132, an all-
**Leyland Lion LT1** has now returned home in its
former Sunderland Corporation livery.

136　Note the typical rounded rear of 1930 in Roe-bodied
　　TF 818, another returned exile **Leyland Lion LT1**
　　from Jersey, now restored to being Lancashire United
　　202 by the L.V.V.S.

137　Platform doors were fitted to TJ 6760, an all-**Leyland
　　Lion LT5A** demonstrator, which entered the fleet of
　　Lytham St. Annes Corporation.

138   Lytham St. Annes No. 44 (BTF 24) is a preserved
gearless **Leyland Lion LT7C** model.

139   At the top of Beachy Head stands Eastbourne Corporation's No. 12 (JK 8418), a 1939 vintage **Leyland
Lion LT9.**

140 Once the pride of Wigan Corporation's fleet EK 8367 is a Santus-bodied **Leyland Tiger TS4** which has escaped a scrapyard fate.

141 With boats strapped to its roof for the 1964 Worthing Regatta is Maidstone & District's DKT 16, a Harrington-bodied **Leyland Tiger TS7.**

142    A **special Leyland Tiger TS8** was WG 9328, a
company-bodied bus working as Alexanders No. P638
at Oban in 1962.

143    Preserved in Colin Shear's West of England Transport
Collection is **Leyland Tiger TS8,** EFJ 666 with its
Craven body. Once Exeter No. 66.

144 On display to the public is **Leyland Badger TA** KW 7604 with its 20-seat Plaxton body. It, along with the **PLSC1 Leyland Lion** KW474, belong to the L.V.V.S.

145 London Transport's No. 521 (DLY 521) was one of the many **Leyland** trolleybuses placed into service just before the Second World War.

146 At the 1962 Brighton Rally is Lord Montague's 1922 vintage **Maxwell** 14-seat charabanc CJ 5052.

147 First a lorry, then a bus and finally a caravan is the story of **Morris-Commercial Leader** WV 8628, awaiting a sponsor at Lincoln.

148　At Lancing, Sussex, is restored **Morris-Commercial**
CKE 64 of 1935.

149　A 26-seat Taylor body is fitted to this preserved **Reo
Pullman** NG 1109.

150 Originally imported from the U.S.A. as a lorry, a bus body was soon fitted to NN 373, an extant **Riker.**

151 A diesel engine altered HA 9483 of Midland Red into a **CON** model **S.O.S.**

152　For many years employed by Trent as a mobile booking office at Skegness, RC 2721 is a preserved **S.O.S. DON** with a Brush body.

153　Working the last route that was abandoned for trolleybus working is another Bournemouth **Sunbeam MS2,** No. 229 (BRU 13).

154 Derby Corporation owned several wartime **Sunbeam W4** trolleybuses such as No. 185 (RC 8885), this one with a utility type Park Royal body.

155 Another **Sunbeam W4,** this time with a Brush body, is Hull's 78 (GRH 298)

**A.D.C. 802.** Pl. 1

Writing in *Buses Illustrated* for February 1964, Alan Townsin exclaimed: 'The LS or "London Six" of 1927-8 occupied a position in the history of the British motor bus not unlike that of the "Great Eastern" in the annals of shipping. Both were considerable achievements by the standards of the times in which they were built and yet neither lived up to the promise they appeared to show when introduced.'

LS1 (YH 1200), the prototype was 29 ft. 1½ ins. long, with a wheelbase of 18 ft. 6 ins. It was powered by a Daimler CV35 Mk. I engine of 35 h.p. and a capacity of 5·7 litres. The 6 cylinders had a bore of 97 mm. and a stroke of 130 mm. The body of LS1 was built by the L.G.O.C. themselves and sat 36 passengers on the top deck and 32 on the lower, a grand total of 68, two short of the number carried on London tramcars at this date. Unlike the tail-enders of the NS class it had a completely enclosed staircase. It started service on route 16 (Victoria–Cricklewood) on 4 June 1927.

The second chassis to be built lived up to the opening remarks of this entry. Working under the trade plate 020 LC, it was used by A.E.C. to transport some of their employees, who lived 20 miles away from the Southall Works in Walthamstow where A.E.C. had formerly been based. Powered by an A.E.C. A121 unit, its L.G.O.C. body seated no less than 59 on the upper deck and 45 on the lower deck, an almost unbelievable total of 104. Presumably, since their daily return journey was free, the squeezed-in occupants could hardly complain of the lack of leg room.

London General's LS2 (YH 1166) followed in August 1927, with an overall length of 29 ft. 5 ins. for its L.G.O.C. 66-seat body, on a wheelbase of 18 ft. 10½ ins. It too had an A.E.C. A121 engine. During the autumn of 1927 there appeared a series of demonstrators all powered by the Daimler CV35 unit. With Short Bros bodywork, they were sent to Maidstone & District (KO 5702), Southdown (UF 2638), Birmingham Corporation (OX 4594) and Sheffield Corporation (WE 2205). However, Westcliff-on-Sea Motor Services actually purchased one outright (HJ 7670). A further A.D.C. 802 became a second A.E.C. Works Bus with a 102-seat body, again using trade plates.

Throughout 1928 a trickle of these giants came off the production lines designed for London General's consumption. All were fitted with Company built bodies. LS3 (UC 2201) and LS12 (YW 8003) had A.E.C. A121 units, but the rest had the Daimler CV35 engine. LS6 (UC 2299) was unique in being the sole 802 to have a single-deck body, and with only 34 seats, this seems rather a puny total for such a large chassis to have carried. The rest had either 70- or 72-seat bodies 29 ft. 11 ins. in length. LS6 spent most of its days working out of Edgware Station on route 104E.

## A.E.C. Y. Pl. 3

The A.E.C. Y was already three years old by the time our story began, but it went on into the early 'twenties and appeared at the 1921 Olympia Show by which time it had been redesigned as the A.E.C. 501. It was also called the A.E.C. 45 h.p., since this was the R.A.C. development rating at 1,000 r.p.m. of its engine, which might have been of A.E.C., Daimler or Tylor manufacture. The A.E.C. unit was a 4 cylinder unit with bore/stroke measurements of 120 mm/150 mm. A 4 speed crash gearbox was fitted and the rear axle was worm-driven.

The chassis came in three weights, 3 ton, 4 ton and 5 ton. Hence it is not surprising that a wide variety of bodies were found attached to the Y, the YC and the 501 chassis. For example Devon General started off in 1919–20 with a motley collection of these. Nos. 1–3 (T 6942/4/6) had 48-seat open top double-deck bodies; Nos. 4/5 (T 7750/2) were rear entrance single-deck buses; T 8232/4 were described as 'lorry buses'; Nos. 6/7 (T 8328/30) had charabanc bodies. Also, down in the West Country Torquay Tramways purchased T 8188–206 (even numbers only!) with 26-seat front entrance bus bodies. Up in Edinburgh the civic authorities during 1920–1 took delivery of a whole series of Ys with Hora 31-seat rear entrance bus bodies (Nos. 156–185). The National Omnibus and Transport Company (based on Chelmsford, Essex) had their Nos. 2001–2006/13/15/16/21/25/29–31 fitted with 44- or 36-seat open top bodies, with 25-, 28-, 29- or 32-seat charabanc bodies, or else as 26- or 32-seat buses. Thus in a mere fourteen vehicles there were eight varieties! Rhondda No. 19 (NY 6327) had quite a high capacity charabanc body seating 35 against Coventry's septet (Nos. 1–7, HP 445/6/8–52) which had 28-seat rear entrance Hora bodyworks, and these were followed by HP 1474 with a 36-seat Hickman bus body.

Some of these chassis had a new lease of life as late as 1927, when A. Timpson & Son re-engined their Ys with new Tylor Tiger JB4 units of 45–50 h.p. rating and with a 5 ins. bore and a 6 ins. stroke. Three such conversions were DY 1401, DY 1761 and DY 1848.

In single-deck work, the 501 was succeeded in 1925–6 by the 411/3 (known as the Renown) and the 412/4 (called the Blenheim), while the double-deck chassis replacement was the S and NS.

**A.E.C. K.** Pl. 4, 5, 53, 54
Although there had been nearly 4,000 A.E.C. B type buses on the streets of London by the outbreak of the Great War, by the time 1919 was reached barely half this number (1,758) had sur-

vived. To replace these and at the same time to try and increase the number of passengers carried on each double-decker the 'K' type was introduced. Instead of 34 passengers this could seat 46. Since A.E.C.'s share capital had been provided by the L.G.O.C., it was that operator's specifications which were taken most notice of, although Torquay Tramways did buy half a dozen of them in 1921 (TA 1004–6/1168–70).

The K had a 28 h.p. engine incorporating 4 cylinders with bore/stroke measurements of 100mm/140mm. When the first went into service on routes 11 and 25 (Victoria–Seven Kings) in August 1919, Londoners found that their centre of gravity was six ins. lower than on the old B class. This had been achieved by altering the springing arrangements. Compared with the B, which had a body looking exactly like that of a horse drawn vehicle, the K had one specifically constructed to suit a motorbus. Hence instead of normal control it can be described as of a 'semi-forward' model. To keep the weight within police regulations three-ply waterproofed birch was used for nearly all body panels and advertisement boards. The next fact seems fantastic but illustrates the complete change of outlook; the number of screws used for the wooden slats on the seats was reduced from 360 to a mere 36. Concurrently, the width of the stairs was increased from 1 ft. 4 ins. to 1 ft. 6 ins. London altogether received a total of 1,109 Ks.

The 301 series (alias the K) was succeeded by the 401 series called the S in 1922. This was basically a larger version of the K, capable of seating 54 passengers. The engine was 4 h.p. more powerful than that which drove the K, the overall length of the bodywork had increased to 24 ft. 7 ins., and the width was now 7 ft. 1 in. In fact some of the 902 buses of the S class in London did receive single-deck bus bodies. Before S1 (which incidentally seated three more passengers, at 57), could go into service there was much heart searching by the traffic authorities, since it exceeded the maximum laden weight permitted, namely 7 tons. Finally it was agreed to raise this limit to $8\frac{1}{2}$ tons, thus enabling the S to operate. The S single-deckers were employed on the Blackwell Tunnel route between Poplar and Greenwich.

**A.E.C. NS.** Pl. 55
When the first A.E.C. 405 appeared in 1923 as the first of London General's NS class, it was to herald the transitional stage from the K and S era to the world more familiar (to us) of the ST, STL and RT of the nineteen-thirties. In fact the difference in external appearance between NS1 and NS 2387 is quite striking. The new model had a 35 h.p. engine and was 25 ft. long and 7 ft. $3\frac{1}{2}$ ins. wide. This enabled 52 passengers, two less than the preceeding S, to be carried, but in comparably more comfort.

The NS had been planned as a covered-top double-decker, which, as is stated in *Fifty Years of A.E.C.* (p. 10): 'with a low centre of gravity achieved by pressed steel side members cranked behind the front axle and over the double-reduction rear axle, allowed the refinements of a single-step platform and the provision of a roof. Imagine, therefore, the reaction of the public when authority decreed that a roof could not be fitted! Production continued, however, with a modified open-topped version until two years and several public outcries later licences were granted for the fully-enclosed vehicle to operate.'

Pneumatic tyres followed in 1928. Twenty-five NS buses (such as NS 2213, YT 4863) were fitted with specially designed top-decks with bucket type seats placed back-to-back at an angle of 45 degrees to the centre of the floor, so that they could work route 108 under the Thames, via the Blackwall Tunnel.

Windscreens were also fitted later to later versions of the NS that were given A.E.C. model numbers 406–10 and 422.

Although the NS evolved with so many 'modern' features, it still retained the chain or spur gearboxes that had existed in the pre-war B class. The last NS was manufactured in 1928.

**A.E.C. 602 Series.** Pl. 2
It was in 1922 that A.E.C. produced their first rather rectangular looking single-deck trolleybus, the 602, which consisted largely of motorbus components. This was succeeded in 1925 by the 603, which had a wheelbase of 10 ft. $8\frac{3}{4}$ ins. and an overall chassis length of 22 ft. $8\frac{1}{4}$ ins. It was powered by a Bull motor rated at 50 h.p., and designed to seat 30 passengers. In 1925 Bradford, having sampled the 602 in the forms of Nos. 523–8 (KU 1160–5) with their Dick-Kerr motors and Bradford Corporation bodywork and Nos. 529–31 (KU 9104–6) with Bull motors and the manufacturers' own bodywork – turned their attention to the 603 of which they ordered four. The first (No. 540, KW 200) had a Strachans body and the remainder (Nos. 541–3, KW 201–3) had A.D.C. bodywork. Bull motors were used in all four.

There was also a double-deck version with a wheelbase of 15 ft. $9\frac{1}{2}$ ins. and which was suitable for 52-seat bodywork. Like the single-deck 603 it had only one motor instead of the pair often provided at this date for larger trolleybuses. Other variations assembled at this time by A.D.C. were the 604 (1927–8), the 605 (1927) and the 607 (1925–6).

**A.E.C. Regent** Pl. 7, 58–64
Thirty-nine years is a long time for a model to keep going, but that is the time gap between the appearance of the Regent Mark I at the 1929 Olympia Show and the continued production of the Regent Mark V in 1968. Needless to say there is little in common between

the two extremes, but it has been a long tale of evolution. This 4 wheeled double-deck chassis was originally called the 661 model and had a wheelbase of 15 ft 6½ ins., its engine was a new 6 cylinder A.E.C. 6·1 litre unit, and in most respects it was really a smaller form of the Renown 6 wheeler.

The Regent Mark I had an appeal for the largest and the smallest operators alike. At one end of the scale the L.G.O.C. and later the L.P.T.B. based three of their double-decker classes on it. First came the ST and this made its debut in 1930 with ST1 being given a Chiswick Works 49-seat body. Over 1,000 STs eventually found their way into the L.P.T.B., out of approximately 2,000 of the so-called 'short wheelbase' versions of the Regent. Some of these started life with the country operators, who ringed the Metropolis such as East Surrey, Lewis Omnibus Co. of Watford and the National Omnibus and Transport Co. of that same Hertfordshire town. Others came from some of the London central area 'pirates' such as Pembroke. Thomas Tilling used them for both their London and their Brighton routes. In the mid-thirties the streets of Hove, Portslade and Rottingdean were full of such vehicles with their open staircases and wooden folding destination boards fore and aft. Up to 1934 they all received London registrations (viz. GJ 2001–12, GK 6199, GN 6200–26, GP 6227–50 and GW 6255–300), but thereafter they came under East Sussex, the last two batches being registered as NJ 3301–5 (Nos. 6301–5) and NJ 4661–3 (Nos. 6308–10).

Other early users of the Regent included Glasgow in 1930 (Nos. 250–74, GE 7282–99/75–81), Exeter in 1930–1 (Nos. 16–30, FJ 7410–5/820–8) and Bournemouth in 1932 (Nos. 62–7, LJ 5800–5). Leeds patronised the Regent by ordering over thirteen consignments, starting with Nos. 40–51 (UG 1027–38) and ending with No. 500 (HUM 421).

During this period the 'long wheelbase' model of the 661 came into service, in 1933 to be exact. This had its wheelbase increased to 16 ft. 3 ins. and hence an overall body length of 26 ft. instead of 25 ft.

In 1935 Maidstone & District took delivery of some of the new 0661 Regents that had been given the A.E.C. 7·7 litre oil engine. Nos. 122–49 (CKE 440–67) had Weymann bodies, which surprisingly enough for this late date, only seated 48 passengers. However, a similar batch came upon the Kentish scene in 1937 (Nos. 91–104, DKT 26–39). Glasgow had many of the 0661 model between 1937 and 1940, with a variety of 56-seat bodyworks by Cowieson (Nos. 435–59, BGA 1–25; Nos. 600–19, BUS 166–85), Weymanns (Nos. 535–99, BUS 101–65; 646–60, CUS 811–25; 724–73, DGB 372–421), Pickering (No. 635, BYS 763) and English Electric (Nos. 636–45, CUS 801–10).

However some operators preferred the quieter petrol engined version. Among the latter were Cheltenham & District, in 1936, with Nos. 7–12 (BAD 27–32) and Eastbourne Corporation in 1938 (Nos. 6–10, JK 7427–31). Yet equally 'select' Torquay had echoed to the sound of Devon General's oil engined Regent replacements for her tramcars as early as 1934 (Nos. 200–23, OD 7487–510). Two small independents in Hampshire patronised the Regent. At the northern edge of that county, Venture of Basingstoke, bought Nos. 26–31 (BOU 696–701) in 1937, with 56-seat Park Royal bodies, and acquired an 'unfrozen' pair in 1942 (Nos. 44/5, ECG 645/6) with Willowbrook bodywork. At the southern extremity Gosport & Fareham Omnibus Company had Park Royal bodied Regents every year from 1936 until 1939, and some of these lasted in active service with their original bodies until the late sixties! They consisted of Nos. 34–7 (BOR 766–9), 38/9 (CAA 700/1), 40/1

(COU 130/1), 42–5 (DAA 848/5–7) and 46/7 (DOR 720/1).

Returning to London Transport, their second Regent class was the STL, which commenced in 1933 with the arrival of L.G.O.C.'s STL1 (GX 5324) which had a 60-seat body. The STL was in reality a long wheelbase 661. Some had rear entrance bodies and others had front entrances; this was particularly so in the case of vehicles like STL 1044 (BPE 221) one of the so-called Godstone class with their 48 seat-lowbridge Weymanns body for use on route 410 (Godstone-Bromley). One STL (BXD 582) started off as orthodox STL 857 in 1935. Later its half-cab front was replaced by an experimental fully-fronted style and it was then renumbered STF 1. In 1938 it was rebuilt to its original design and it then rejoined the STL ranks as No. 1167. Forty STLs, between Nos. 1809 and 1884, had special upper-decks so that they could negotiate Blackwall Tunnel in place of the ageing NS tunnel buses. By the cessation of production at Southall, this class had reached No. 2647 (FXT 95). However, in 1942, the Ministry of Supply let the L.P.T.B. have a further collection of Regents, which became STL 2648–81 (FXT 371–404). Sixteen of these received wartime 'utility' standard bodies and the remaining eighteen acquired bodies from earlier members of the class. All the STL vehicles were powered by the A.E.C. 7·7 litre diesel engine, apart from the Godstone buses (Nos. 1044–55), which had the stronger 8·8 litre oil unit.

The third London class, based on the Regent, was the RT. The prototype had begun life in London Transport in 1938, as ST1140 (EYK 396), with a 56-seat Leyland body removed from TD 118. However in July 1939 it was given a new style body and was renumbered RT1. Before production ceased in 1940, RT 2–151 (FXT 177–326), had entered service. In effect these buses were early Regent Mark IIIs, since they had 9·6 litre

engines developing 115 b.h.p. London Transport built their own 56-seat bodies for RT 2–151.

**A.E.C. 661T.** Pl. 65, 66

An electrical version of the Regent 661 known as the 661T (T for Trolleybus) appeared in 1931, two years after the debut of the petrol engined model. Its original wheelbase was 15 ft. 6½ ins. and this meant that a 25-ft. double-decker body could be fitted. Outwardly, the 661T looked very much like any other Regent, for it even had a standard radiator. Photographs of early vehicles such as Bournemouth's experimental No. 70 (LJ 7703) with its 50-seat English Electric body, or Notts & Derby Traction's Nos. 317–31 (RB 8951–65) with their 55-seat M.C.W. bodies, are difficult to recognise as trolleybuses at first sight until you notice the trolley booms. Fully fronted styles seem to have started, as far as the 661T is concerned, with the 1934 L.P.T.B. No. 63 (AXU 189) with its English Electric 60-seat body and Portsmouth Corporation's Nos. 1–4 (RV 4649–52) with English Electric 50-seat bodies. Portsmouth followed up this initial batch with Nos. 17–24 (RV 6374–82) in 1935, Nos. 25–54 (RV 8307–36) in 1936 and Nos. 55–100 (RV 9106–54) in 1937. The latter two batches had Craven 52-seat bodywork. In 1936 Reading Corporation tried out its first 661T (No. 2, RD 8086) fitted with a Park Royal 52-seat lowbridge body.

In 1933 the Regent long wheelbase model appeared on the market with an extension of the wheelbase to 16 ft 3 ins. and of the overall body length to 26 ft. The same trends were observable in the 661T trolleybus. In 1937 Notts & Derby took delivery of a further septet of 661Ts (Nos. 300–5/32, DRB 616–32), this time with 56-seat Weymann bodies. For the builders at Southall 1939 was a busy time; not only did Reading decide that their initial vehicle was a success and order a fair sized batch their Nos. 107–131 (ARD 670–94), on this occasion with 56-seat highbridge bodywork), but Hastings Tramways Company began to replace their original fleet of Guy trolleybuses with 661Ts. By the outbreak of the Second World War the number had reached twenty; Nos. 1–10 (BDY 776–85) had 54-seat Weyman bodies and the remaining ten (BDY 786–95) received similar Park Royal bodies. At the same time, trams along the coast at Brighton were being replaced mainly by trolleybuses. Brighton Corporation themselves placed into service by August 1939, Nos. 1–44 (FUF 1–44) with Weyman 54-seat bodies and their partners in this enterprise Brighton, Hove & District Omnibus Company received their eight 661Ts soon after hostilities had started. Nos. 6340–47 (BPN 340–47) were therefore stored until 1945 when they were re-registered with CPM numbers.

Most of the 661Ts appear to have been given English Electric motors. For example, L.P.T.B. 63 was powered by a 406A1 model, Bournemouth 70 by a DE403A unit and Reading 2 worked off a 406/3E type. Brighton operators, however, patronised local industry by purchasing motors and electrical equipment from Crompton-Parkinson and Allan-West.

Similar in size to the Portsmouth collection of 661Ts was the one belonging to Bradford Corporation. Between 1934 and 1938 they assembled quite a muster of these vehicles, all driven by English Electric 405 motors. English Electric bodies were also fitted to Nos. 597–617 (KY 8200–20), 518–32 (AAK 420–34), 634 (BAK 934) and 635–76 (CAK 635–76). After the Second World War Bradford bought second-hand some of the last 661Ts built. Of 1941–2 vintage were ex-Notts & Derby HNU 826–30/970–4.

Not so many of the 662T single-deck

trolleybuses were built for home consumption, but Notts & Derby did buy ten of these in 1932, fitted with English Electric 32-seat front entrance bodies. Nos. 306–15 (RB 6613–22) looked very like contemporary A.E.C. Regals.

## A.E.C. Renown. Pl. 67

In 1929 A.E.C. introduced the 6 wheeled Renown model 663 with its 16 ft. 6 ins. wheelbase and powered by a 6 cylinder A.E.C. engine of 6·1 litres, with bore/stroke dimensions of 100 mm/130 mm. Transmission was by a single plate clutch and a 4 speed sliding mesh gearbox to underslung worm-driven rear axles. Braking was by means of three servo assistance. Of the 1,596 Renowns produced, no less than 1,440 of them went to London General and London Transport as their LT and LTC classes.

The first 663 type Renown was L.G.O.C. LT1 (UU 6611), which entered service on route 16A (Victoria – Cricklewood) in August 1929. This had a Company built 56-seater body that retained the open staircase. It was several months later before LT2–50 appeared on active service, and these looked similar to LT1, but seated 4 more passengers. In August 1930 the first LT with an enclosed staircase came into service on route 121A, at Nunhead Garage. This was LT1000, which had a chassis built at the L.G.O.C's own Chiswick Works. Contemporary with these early London vehicles was Northampton Corporation's No. 40 (VV 119), whose strange looking Grose body seated only 54.

In 1930 there emerged on the scene a lengthened version of the Renown, known as the 664 model. This had a wheelbase of 18 ft. 7 ins., which enabled 30 ft. bodies to be fitted. Two of the first 664s to be manufactured went to Warrington Corporation (ED 5880/1). Due to the fact that they were dual entrance/exit buses they seated only 59. However when L.G.O.C. started taking delivery of the longer model their rear entrance bodies sat 66. Before these appeared, LT 1001–50 had made their debut with 35-seater single-deck bodies. Some of the LT class were fitted with a more powerful petrol engine of 7·4 litres, in which the bore had been increased to 110 mm, but the real breakthrough came with LT 191–99 in the spring of 1931, for these had 6 cylinder 8·097 litre diesel units with 110 mm bore and 142 mm stroke. There followed several different types of A.E.C. oil engines such as the A161, the A164 and the more famous 8·8 litre A165; LT 1417–26 received the Gardner 6LW engine, which was put into LT 741 in place of its earlier A.E.C. unit.

With a 58-seat Short Bros. body, Birmingham purchased a 663 demonstrator as their No. 92 (MV 489) and Glasgow tried out one with a 60-seat Cowieson body (No. 50, GG 4681). Doncaster bought one 663 in 1934 (No. 66, DT 5337) and a further four in 1935 (DT 6100–3). All had 60 seat Roe bodyworks. The maximum seating capacity, 66 passengers, of any 664, was reserved for a pair that went to Ebor Bus Company of Mansfield (VO 7884/5) and a quartet that entered the fleet of Eastern National (Nos. 3332–5, MJ 406/7 and 290/1). The latter had lowbridge bodies built by Strachans.

Some of the last Renowns to operate were those of Leicester Corporation. Nos. 321–9 (CBC 913–21) came in 1938 with 64-seat Northern Counties bodies; Nos. 330–45 (DBC 221–36) with M.C.W. bodywork followed two years later and must have been amongst the last 664s to be built. Incidentally, the 663 had ceased production in 1937.

Perhaps the strangest of all the Renowns was LT1137 (GP 3456) of 1931, which was the prototype double-deck Green Line coach. It had a front entrance, but for many years combined this with rear stairs! Its 50-seat body

with coach style seating also possessed that popular feature of the 'thirties, a folding 'sunshine' roof. For their private hire work, L.P.T.B. purchased the LTC class in 1937. These were on O663 chassis, and EGO 505–28 had front entrance 32-seat bodies constructed by Weymanns.

## A.E.C., 663T. Pl. 68–72

Just as the 661T was the trolleybus form of the Regent and the 662T the trolleybus version of the Regal, so the Renown was found in the shape of the 663T trolleybus as from 1930. This chassis could carry a body of 27 ft. in length and was a 6 wheel model. The prototype-demonstrator, bearing an English Electric 53-seat lowbridge body, was sold in 1932 to Southend Corporation and became their No. 116 (JN 2086). Perhaps the most famous set of 663Ts ever built were the so-called 'Diddlers' of London United Tramways, which became London's first regular trolleybuses in 1931. L.U.T's subsidiary, Union Construction, built their 56-seat rear entrance bodies, each bearing a distinctive single headlamp at the front which gave them quite the air of a tram The first batch (Nos. 1–35, with an assortment of HX registrations) were powered by English Electric DK 130A motors and the remainder (Nos. 36–60, with assorted MG registrations) relied on B.T.H. 110DL motors. A sixty-first vehicle (No. 61, AHX 801) received an experimental L.G.O.C. 74-seat central entrance body in 1933. The newly formed London Passenger Transport Board, after taking into stock No. 62 (AXU 188) with its rear entrance 73-seat M.C.W. body in 1934, began placing massive orders for the 663T with a variety of bodywork but powered mainly by the English Electric 406A motor. Between 1935 and 1937 the L.P.T.B. received A.E.Cs., with bodywork seating 70 passengers, from Weymanns (Nos. 132–141, CGF 132, etc.; 604–28, DLY

604, etc.), from M.C.W. (Nos. 142–83, CGF 142, etc.; 184–283, CUL 184, etc.) and the Birmingham Railway Carriage Works (Nos. 284–383, CUL 284, etc.). All the above mentioned were of the newer and longer 664T model where the overall length had been increased to 30 ft. From 1938 until the war halted production in 1940, London Transport received further consignments of the 664T, this time powered by Metro-Vick 206A3 motors. Apart from a solitary M.C.W. bodied trolleybus (No. 952, ELB 952) the work of body building was shared between Weymanns (Nos. 905–51, ELB 905, etc.), Park Royal (Nos. 629–53, DLY 629, etc.; 1645–69, FXH 645, etc.) and B.R.C.W. (Nos. 955–99, ELB 955, etc.; 1000, EXX 10; 1001–54, EXV 1–54; 1555–644, FXH 555, etc.).

Before the 663T disappeared from the scene in 1939 it had found its way into several other fleets. Birmingham bought five in 1932 fitted with 58-seat Short Bros. bodies (Nos. 12–16, OJ 1012–16), whilst in 1933 another of Bournemouth's trial trolleybuses was a 663T (No. 69, LJ 7702). Portsmouth bought a brace of 663Ts in 1934 with 60-seat bodies by English Electric (No. 12, RV 4658) and M.C.W. (No. 15, RV 4663). Walsall Corporation also tried out a pair in 1931 (Nos. 151/2, DH 8311/2) fitted with English Electric 60-seat bodies.

Some of the last 664T trolleybuses built went to Cardiff in 1941 to start their new system; Nos. 201–10 (CKG 191–200) had Northern Counties 70 seat rear entrance bodies and were powered by English Electric motors.

## A.E.C. Reliance. Pl. 6

In 1928 A.E.C. decided to give the A.D.C. 426, a 6 cylinder engine in place of its 4 cylinder unit, thus creating the first A.E.C. model to bear the name Reliance. This new engine was a 6·1 litre one with a bore of 100 mm and a stroke of 130 mm. It developed 95 b.h.p. at 2,500 r.p.m. A rather old-fashioned feature was the cone clutch which operated the D118 sliding mesh gearbox. The Reliance was provided with fully-floating rear axles.

Designated the 660, the Reliance retained the 426's wheelbase measurement of 16 ft. Three prototypes entered service in November with J. Sharp (Manchester), Brown Bros. (Sapcote, Leices.) and East Surrey Traction Company (No. 78, PK 4243). The latter was fitted with a Hall Lewis body with a rear entrance and a front emergency exit. Of the 484 Reliance chassis built, the largest batch went to the L.N.E.R. who were developing feeder bus routes for their lines, especially in East Anglia. Their share consisted of seventy-four of the 660s. The biggest municipal order for this model came from Nottingham Corporation, whose twenty Short Bros. bodied Reliances bore Middlesex registrations (viz. MY 534–43/775–7/836–42) as they were licensed before leaving the Southall Works. Edinburgh Corporation took fourteen Reliances fitted with dual entrance/exit Croall bodies seating 32 as their Nos. 774–87 (SC 3417–30) and in Ireland G.N.R. took delivery of twenty 660s with similar seating arrangements (Nos. 14, 22–32 and 39–46).

Royal Blue of Bournemouth had taken some of the last 426s built in 1928. These Hall Lewis bodied coaches (RU 7730–5) had the new 6 cylinder A130 engine installed in place of their original 4 cylinder A127 units in November 1929, thus converting them into A.D.C. 426/6, although in reality they were as much Reliances as Royal Blue's 1929 consignment consisting of RU 8801–25. The London General bought thirty-nine Reliances to form their R class. The last Reliances were built at the beginning of 1932.

## A.E.C. Regal. Pl. 56–57

Introduced at the same time as the 661 Regent and the 663 Renown, was the

662 Regal, a 4 wheel, 6 cylinder engined single-decker. Indeed, apart from having a wheelbase of 17 ft., it resembled the original Regent in most respects. London General were one of the first major operators to see the benefit of buying Regals and straightway, in 1929, they took delivery of forty-six of these as the foundation of their new T class (UU 6616-61). Each had a front entrance L.G.O.C. body seating 30 passengers. Transmission was through a normal clutch and a crash gearbox.

Another early employer of the first model Regal was Rhondda who took into their ranks, in 1930, six of these new vehicles fitted with Park Royal 30-seat rear entrance bodies. Nos. 66–71 had odd numbered registrations (viz. TG 743/5/7/9/51/5). Amongst others who sampled the new 662 but did *not* follow this up with big orders, were Leeds Corporation (Nos. 28–33, UG 1021–6), Exeter Corporation (No. 15, FJ 7463) and Royal Blue (LJ 650 and LJ 1510–8).

In 1933, as in the case of the Regent, the wheelbase was lengthened to 17 ft. 6 ins., which at 27 ft. 6 ins. added an extra eighteen inches to the overall dimensions of the bodywork. At the same time fully-floating rear axles replaced the former semi-floating variety. Lockheed hydraulic brakes were also a new feature of the Regal from that date. Some Regals were now receiving the A.E.C. A165 Ricardo type oil engine of 8·8 litres with a bore of 115 mm and a stroke of 142 mm, developing 130 b.h.p. at 2,000 r.p.m. This was replaced in 1936 by the smaller so-called 7·7 litre diesel engine (actually its capacity was 7·58 litres) with a bore of 105 mm and a stroke of 146 mm which at first, as the A171 in 1934, developed 108 b.h.p. at 2,000 r.p.m., but later was derated to 95 b.h.p. at 1,800 r.p.m. (the A173 unit). In either form it was known as the 0662 model. This had a conventional friction clutch and crash gearbox, although some versions had a

fluid flywheel and a Wilson self-changing gearbox.

London Transport, in 1937, bought fifty of the 0662 model, the first single-deckers that they had ordered since their formation four years earlier. T 403–52 (CLX 551–75 and CXX 151–75) had Weymann 31-seat bodies and were powered by the A173 unit. There followed a year later 266 more 0662s in the huge fleet, this time with either 31- or 34-seat L.P.T.B. bodyworks. T 453–718 (ELP 177–289 and EYK 201–353) had the 8·8 litre engine along with the fluid flywheel transmission. At this time Devon General were also taking the 0662 in the form of 32- or 35-seat front entrance buses (Nos. 401–17, 420–51, 454–79). Strange to relate, Bristol Tramways at this juncture, decided to supplement their supply of Jo5Gs and L5Gs with some 6 cylinder Regals with Park Royal bodywork (Nos. 2092–2109, EHW 442–59; 2215–34, GL 5039/40/56–60/ 73–85; 2235/6, GL 1510/1). Walker bodies were fitted to Aberdeen's collection of Regals, built up over the period 1936–9.

Between 1931 and 1936 a 4 cylinder version of the Regal, known as the 642 Regal 4, was built in small numbers. This could be either a petrol or a diesel unit. Gosport & Fareham Omnibus Company bought eight that were replaced only in 1968 (Nos. 23–30, CG 9606/7/10–13/08/9). Originally they all had 32-seat rear entrance Harrington bodies. Dublin United Tramways built their own bodies for Nos. 396 (ZI 9709), 431–40 (ZA 983–92), 453–64 (ZA 1977–86), 540–4 (ZA 1988–92), 643–52 (ZA 3859–68) and 685–94 (ZA 3879–88).

Yet another version was the Regal Mark II, designated the 0862, which flourished from 1936 until 1939. Perhaps 'flourished' is inapt, since few were in demand. Its small 6 cylinder oil engine (bore 105 mm, stroke 130 mm) was designed to occupy only the room taken up by the unit in the 642 model. Rhondda bought some in 1936 (Nos. 11, ATG 515; 12, ATX 414; 14–20, ATG 516–22) equipped with 34-seat Weyman bodies, and G.N.R. No. 61 (ZA 7156) had a Company built 35-seat body. P.M.T. tried out No. 100 (CVT 34), whose Burlingham body sat 39 passengers.

## A.E.C. Ranger

In 1930 a normal control version of the Regal was introduced and numbered the 665. The Ranger was mainly aimed at the export market and was manufactured for these overseas customers until 1938. In Britain, however, it found few clients. Burton-on-Trent Corporation purchased a solitary one in 1934, No. 44 (FA 5449) fitted with a Brush 26-seat front entrance bus body. More common was the use of the Rangers for extended tours. Devon General bought two lots three years apart for their Grey Cars subsidiary. In 1935 they took delivery of Nos. 334/5 (AUO 199/8) which carried 26-seat rear entrance Harrington coach bodies, and in 1938 they put into service, Nos. 346–53 (ETT 985–92) with front entrance coach bodies by the Hove builder. Another Ranger with a Craven coach body (AWJ 233) found its way in 1934 into the fleet of Smith's Tours of Waterhouses. As you can see, the relatively backward position of the driver meant a sacrifice of some 6 seats and this made the 665 an uneconomic vehicle to operate.

## A.E.C. Q Single-decker. Pl. 75, 76

On 5 September 1932 Londoners riding on route 11E (Shepherds Bush–Liverpool Street), were rather startled to see a strange new single-decker operating. This was the L.G.O.C's No. Q 1 (GX 5395) which had been especially designed for them in conjunction with A.E.C. It was called the Q since in the First World War this letter was used for 'hush-hush' ships that were still in their experimental stage. Q 1 had a body built at Chiswick and seated 37 with an entrance immediately to the rear of the front axle. However, it was not the fully-fronted appearance of the Q that attracted attention, so much as the position of its engine which was situated on the offside behind the front axle. This was a 6 cylinder A.E.C. petrol unit. The Q 1 was 27 ft. long and 7 ft. 6 ins. wide.

It was during 1935 and 1936 that London Transport began to receive production Qs from A.E.C. with 37-seat bodies constructed by the Birmingham Railway Carriage and Wagon Company. They entered the Country Area as Q 6–55 (BXD 527–76), Q 56–105 (CGJ 161–210) and Q 186/7 (CLE 127/8). Their transmission was the standard L.P.T.B. hydraulic system and the power came from an A.E.C. 7·7 litre indirect-injection oil engine. The gap consisting of Q 106–185 (CLE 129–208) was made up of a version with a shorter wheelbase, for use in the Central Area. The entrance was forward of the front axle, but the Park Royal bodies still seated 37. Finally, at the close of 1936 came a batch of Park Royal coach bodies seating 32 and which were intended for use on the Green Line network. Q 189–238 (CXX 382–406/DGX 220–244) were placed on routes M1 and M3 (Hertford–Guildford), M2 (Hertford–West Byfleet), H3 (Luton–Kings Cross), Q (High Wycombe–London) and R (Chesham–London). Despite the fewer seats these members of the L.P.T.B. Q class had the longer wheelbase, with the entrance situated behind the front axle.

Among the early users of the single-deck version of the Q was Elliotts of Bournemouth, who ran the Royal Blue express coaches. Their quartet of LJ 8001, LJ 8600, LJ 8601 and AEL 2 had 37-seat Duple bodies with central entrances. Eventually they became Nos. 618–21 in the Hants & Dorset fleet. North of the Border, Dundee Corporation had a trio of Weyman 37-seat central entrance buses (Nos. 1–3, YJ 2800–2), and Aberdeen tried out no less than eleven, fitted with rear entrance (a rare feature with this model) Walker bus bodies seating 39 (Nos. 21–31, RG 5021/5622–31). Edinburgh contented themselves with a solitary 38-seat Weyman with a front entrance (WS 1508). Quite a plethora of Q were to be found in South Wales, in the ranks of Gelligaer U.D.C. (TG 6266 and BTX 113), Gough's Welsh Motorways of Mountain Ash (AAX 826/7 and ATX 338), Imperial Motor Services (TG 8499, TG 9953, ATG 307, ATG 835, ATX 937, BAX 141 and BTG 139) and finally South Wales itself (Nos. 360–5, WN 8260–5). Some independents purchased coach versions of the Q and the pair that worked for Suttons of Clacton (BNO 228/9) had Duple front entrance bodies that sat only 29, presumably in considerable comfort.

## A.E.C. Q Double-decker

In 1934 London Transport took delivery of a pair of experimental double-deckers based on the Q single-decker chassis. They were given A.E.C. 6 cylinder petrol engines which were fitted on the offside at the rear of the front axle. Q 2 (AYV 615) and Q 3 (AYV 616) had 56-seat Metro-Cammell high-bridge type bodies, with a front entrance forward of the front axle. They were placed in service on route 114 (Mill Hill to South Harrow). Another pair (Q4, BPG 507 and Q 5, BPJ 224) were similar in chassis details to the previous two mentioned, but their 56-seat Weymann bodies had central entrances with air-operated sliding doors. They began their working life on route 406 (Reigate–Kingston) in August 1934.

A number of Q double-deckers were built and ended up in a variety of municipal and independent fleets such as AML 663 with Grimsby Corporation, AML 996 and UG 6511 with Leeds Corporation and HF 9401 and 9399 with Wallasey Corporation. Worth's of Enstone, Oxfordshire, gathered together four Qs but this was rather an exception to the general rule.

Unique among the Q double-deckers was L.P.T.B. Q 188 (DGO 500), which had three axles, was designed to take a 51-seat double-deck coach body constructed by Park Royal, and was scheduled for duty on the Aldgate–Grays Green Line route. It had a 7·7 litre A.E.C. petrol engine, transmission being via an electrically operated Cotal gearbox, and a central entrance, but proving too sluggish for swifter coach duties it finally entered service on Country Area route 340, operating out of Hertford garage in 1938.

There was a 761 T version of the Q, for trolleybus duties. Only five were built; one went to Bradford Corporation (633, KY 6210) and one to Southend Corporation (223, JN 4373). The latter had a 56-seat English Electric body. Two went to Australian customers. KY 6210 was sold, and entered the fleet of South Shields Corporation (No. 235) as late as 1942. This had a 63-seat English Electric body.

## Albion PB24 Series

Writing in *Buses Illustrated* for July 1952, John G. Gilham remarked that: 'During the late 'twenties the vast majority of buses throughout Scotland, whether owned by large companies, municipalities, or independents, were made by Albion, but after most of these private operators were consolidated under single ownership, the new group began to purchase most of its chassis in Lancashire.'

Thus in 1926, Albions of Scotstoun, Glasgow, began to manufacture a new range of low loader single-deck chassis. Those bearing the suffix 24 were powered by an Albion 24 h.p. engine with bore of $3\frac{7}{8}$ in. and stroke of 5 in.; those with the suffix 26 had a larger 30/60 engine (i.e. R.A.C. rating of 30 h.p., developing 60 b.h.p. at the optimum revolutions per minute). This unit had a bore of $4\frac{5}{16}$ in. and a stroke of $4\frac{3}{4}$ in. The easiest way to explain the variations is to tabulate them:

| Model | Wheelbase | Seats |
|-------|-----------|-------|
| PB 24 | 11 ft. 3 ins. | 14 |
| PH 24 | 14 ft. | 20 |
| PJ 24 | 14 ft. | 24 |
| PJ 26 | 14 ft. 4 ins. | 25 |
| PK 26 | 16 ft. | 29 |

All these models incorporated normal control, but by the 1927 Commercial Motor Show a forward control version had been introduced, the PM28, which with a wheelbase of 16 ft. 3 ins. could seat 32. This was driven by the 30/60 unit. Meanwhile, the normal control series was further added to by the appearance of the PFB 26 (wheelbase 15 ft.; seats 20) and the PNA26 (wheelbase 16 ft. 3 ins.; seats 26). Front wheel brakes were fitted to the PFB26.

Kilmarnock Corporation bought a pair of PH24s in 1924 and had 19 seat bus bodies placed on SD 8799/800. Aberdeen were interested in the PJ24 and bought one with a 25-seat front entrance body in 1926 (No. 35, HS 4104), followed by rear entrance versions in 1927 (Nos. 37–45, RS 8051–65) and 1928 (Nos. 46–55, RS 8985–94). The bigger PM28 went to Glasgow Corporation in 1927 (Nos. 19/20, GD 7558/9) and 1928 (Nos. 21–30, GD 9716–25), all carrying 32-seat rear entrance Cowieson bodywork. Great Southern Railway, of Eire, bought several of a new model of the PM28 brought out in 1929 and known as the PMA28. This improved model also bore the name Viking. ZI 1898–1900/39–41/2012/20–24 all had 32-seat front entrance bodywork. In Wales, Rhondda had Brush bodies fitted to their PMA28s Nos. 61–3 (TX 9227/3/5) and 64/5 (TX 9858/60) in 1930. The PMB28 was called the Viking Six since it was powered by a 6 cylinder engine. In this stronger form it found favour with Edinburgh Corpora-

tion who tried out SC9902 with an Alexanders dual entrance/exit body; Rhondda also bought a pair as their Nos. 58/9 (TX 8715/3) with Brush 32-seat bodywork.

Meanwhile the PK26 had been replaced by the improved PKA26 (which was also called the Viking to add to the confusion!). However, to add to the plethora of letters and numbers, the first of the 6 cylinder Viking Sixes were actually the PNC26 (a normal control 26-seater) and the PR28 (a forward control 32-seater). In 1930 the PNC26 gave place to the PKB26. This range of vehicles was ousted in 1932 by the new Valiant line.

**Albion Victor.** Pl. 9, 81

The normal control Victor appeared in the Albion catalogues from 1931. Basically it was a 20-seater and therefore it replaced the former PH24. The original model was styled the PH49 and was itself replaced in 1934 by an improved version, the PHB49. At the same time, a slightly larger form, the PHA49, designed to seat 24 passengers, was introduced, as well as an even bigger one called the PH111 with a seating capacity of 26.

Perhaps because they found competition with the Leyland Cub and the Dennis Ace too great, Albions now began to concentrate more on a medium sized single-decker with their PH115 Victor in 1935. This was a 26-seat normal control model partnered by the first forward control Victor, the PK115. Because of the driver's revised seat position, it was possible to fit an extra half dozen seats into this version. Burwell & District saw fit to buy one of the PH115 variety as their No. 17 (CCE 768). This vehicle was designed in the form of a coach. Union Jack asked Strachans to build them a 32-seat front entrance coach body for their PK115 (ANM 532). In Essex, PK115s appeared with many different bodies. For example, HNO 907 and HVK 221 had Thurgood bodies, FHK 199 a Waveney one, and DNO 837 and EVW 868 had Duple bodies.

In 1936 24- (PH114) and 28-seat (PK114) models were added to the list All the 114s and 115s had the Albion 3·88 litre petrol engine, although Premier Travel of Cambridge did equip their PK114 (No. 9, CUR 921) with a Perkins 4 cylinder oil unit.

## Albion Valiant

In 1932 the Valiant was presented by Albions as a replacement for the Viking Six. In its original form it was known as the PV70 and had a 6 cylinder unit with a bore/stroke of 4 in./4$\frac{7}{8}$ in. Two years later an oil engine of a similar capacity, and manufactured by Albions themselves, was offered as an alternative. In 1935 an improved model of the Valiant, the PV71, appeared. Union Jack acquired a PV70 demonstrator with a Cowieson 32-seat body (GG 5821) and followed this up by ordering, in 1934, one of their own (MJ 4350). In the same year Burwell & District sampled a 32-seater coach version of the PV70 (No. 12, ACE 764). Red & White, whose headquarters were at Chepstow, Monmouthshire, began to buy many Albions in the mid-'thirties. In 1935 they purchased the PV71 that had been exhibited at that year's Olympia Show and this became No. 260. This operator also ran some SP71 models (with oil engines?) under the legend of one of their subsidiaries Liberty Motors of Cardiff (Nos. 301-7).

In 1937 the PV71 was replaced by the PV141 which then took the name of Valkyrie.

## Albion Valkyrie. Pl. 78

The first Valkyrie appeared in the form of the PX65 in 1931. This was a 32-seater single-decker powered by a 4 cylinder petrol engine. The following

year the PW65 was introduced which, as the result of an extended wheelbase, could seat 36 passengers. The variations of a different radiator and a slight advancement of the cab-front brought into being in 1934, the PW67 model. This was given either an Albion 4 cylinder petrol engine (bore 4$\frac{5}{8}$ in.; stroke 5$\frac{1}{2}$ in.) or else the Gardner 4LW or 5LW oil engines. In 1935 there came a further variation, the PW69, which was basically an extended form of the PW67, but which could carry 39 seated passengers. There was a choice of 3 engines as in the case of the PW67.

In 1932 Highland Omnibuses bought a pair of PW65s with their own 32-seat front entrance bodies fitted (Nos. 9/10, ST 6982/3), and this order was followed up in 1934 with one for three PW67 models (Nos. 59-61, ST 7762-4) bearing Highland's own 34-seat rear entrance bodywork. A fourth PW67 (No. 62, ST 8029) followed the next year. Aberdeen Corporation had some 35-seat Walker bodied PW69s in 1935 (Nos. 32-4/6-40, RG 5632, etc.).

In 1937 a new form of the Valkyrie entered the market. This time there was a choice of 2 engines. The PV141 had a 6 cylinder 7·82 unit with a bore of 4$\frac{1}{2}$ in. and a stroke of 5 in., while the PW141 had a 4 cylinder 6·06 litres unit with a bore of 4$\frac{5}{8}$ in. and a stroke of 5$\frac{1}{2}$ in. Since the 4 cylinder engine did not take up as much space the PW141 was designed to seat 39, compared with 35 for the PV141. A further variation was asked for by some operators, such as Highland, and this produced the SPW141 (S for Special) which had a Gardner 5LW diesel engine instead of either of the two petrol choices. These vehicles were numbered 68/9 (ST 8652/1) of 1936 vintage, 73 (ST 9132) of 1937, and 80 (ST 9612) of 1938.

Two 6 wheeler versions of the Valkyrie were produced in 1936-7 which had forward control and seated up to 44 passengers. The 6 cylinder engine was fitted to the PR145 and the 4 cylinder unit to the PW145. Again Highland took a diesel engined SPW145 in 1938, No. 79 (ST 9767), which had a company built 40-seat rear entrance body.

A new generation of Valkyries began to appear in 1938 and for them a new system of numbering was devised. According to the type of engine desired so the seating varied. Thus, the CX9 model with its 4 cylinder Albion engine and the CX11 model with its Gardner 5LW 7·00 litre unit, were designed to cope with 39 passengers seated. On the other hand the CX13 had either the Albion 6 cylinder 9·08 litre engine or the Gardner 6LW 8·40 litre unit, and could only seat 36. All three shared the old PV141/PW141 chassis. Highland continued its patronage of the Valkyrie by taking delivery of Nos. 81 (ST 9978), 82 (AST 100) and 100 (AST 734) with 33 seats, 38 seats and 36 seats respectively. Highland also bought a CX13 (No. 91, AST 505) fitted with their own 35 seat body. In 1939 Glasgow Corporation had a batch of Valkyries described as CX25s, obviously a specialised version for that municipality. Nos. 686–92 (CUS 851–7) had Pickering 35-seat front entrance bodies.

**Albion Venturer.** Pl. 79
In 1933 GG9600, a demonstrator double-decker with a 51-seat Brush body, and known as the Venturer, appeared. Eventually GG9600 was bought by Union Jack. When the type 80 Venturer went into production the following year, it was designed to seat four passengers more than the prototype, and it was powered by a 6 cylinder petrol engine with a 4¼ in. bore and a 5 in. stroke. In 1935 there was a new version of the Venturer known as the type 81. This had a Gardner 6LW engine. Glasgow Corporation bought twenty of these in a special form called the SP81, and had

Cowieson 52-seat bodies built for Nos. 1–20 (YS 2001–20) in 1935. Later they ordered another thirty this time referred to as M81s, Nos. 21–50 (YS 2081–2110).

1938 saw the emergence of the CX19 model with its Albion 6 cylinder 9·08 litre oil engine. This had a bore of 117·4 mm and a stroke of 139·7 mm and developed 102 b.h.p. at 1,750 r.p.m. The Gardner 6LW continued to be an option. Between 1938 and 1942 Glasgow took delivery of a considerable number of these 56-seat Venturers. Some (Nos. 620–34, BUS 186–200) had Cowieson bodywork, others had Pickering bodies (Nos. 666–85, CUS 831–50; 804–23, DGB 452–71; 824/5, DGB 440/1); English Electric supplied the bodies of some of the 1939 consignment (Nos. 661–5, CUS 826–30), M.C.W. some of the 1940 batch (Nos. 774–83, DGB 422–31), and finally the Corporation themselves undertook this work for wartime Nos. 784–91 (DGB 432–9). Red & White tried out two Venturers in 1939, No. 399 (CAX 399) with a Duple body and No. 419 (CWO 419) with a Weyman body. Cheltenham & District bought CX19s with M.C.W. bodywork in 1940 (Nos. 29–33, EAD 729–33).

A solitary 6 wheeled version of the Venturer named the Valorous was built in 1934 and began duty in the fleet of Young's Bus Services of Paisley (No. 71, GG 9462).

**Bedford WHB.** Pl. 81–83
In July 1931 a new coach for J. Woodham of Melchbourne was completed at Vauxhall's Luton Works and at Duple's Hendon Works, and on 31 August this Bedford operator took delivery of TM 9547, chassis No. 1000001, the very first Bedford coach ever built. When this WHB was withdrawn from active service in 1956 it seemed doomed to end its life on a Cambridgeshire farm until, in 1960,

Arlington Motors of Bedford took charge of and beautifully restored it and it now appears at many rallies, incidentally proving to be a useful advertisement for this Bedford agent.

The WHB was a normal control 6 cylinder vehicle with a 3·18 litre petrol engine, transmission being through a single plate clutch and a 4 speed gearbox. The wheelbase was only 10ft. 11 in. and it was designed to take a 14-seater body. This began the partnership with Duples that has resulted in many of the 55,000 Bedford coaches produced since 1931 having bodies of this make. A mere 102 of the WHB were only ever constructed, all but eight being for home consumption, before it ceased to be built in May 1933. Among the few operators of this first Bedford model was Winchester & District who used a pair with bus bodies on some of their local routes. They were registered as CG 19 and CG 20.

About the time that TM 9547 was undergoing manufacture a demonstrator of a larger version, the WLB, was also being made ready. MV 8996 had a wheelbase of 13 ft. 1 in. which enabled a Duple 20-seat coach body to be fitted. Two years later Howards of West Byfleet, Surrey, purchased this vehicle for their West Byfleet Station – Pyrford Hospital Service. It was so employed until the mid sixties when it was bought for preservation by Mr. Don Teesdale, the chairman of the Lincolnshire Vintage Vehicle Society. Altogether 1,431 of the 1,895 WLBs built were sold in Britain, the last appearing in September 1935. Most of them went to small owner-drivers, but Exeter Corporation ran one (No. 41, FJ 9000), as did the local branch of the Transport & General Workers Union at Littleport, Cambs. (JE 23). Although most had Duple 20-seat front entrance coach bodywork, Quest Motors of Essex had an Economy (of Ipswich) body fixed to AHK 611 and Union Jack

(Luton) used MJ 7021 which incorporated a Strachan bus body.

As from January 1935 a new model, the WTB, appeared. This was basically the 27 h.p. WLB but with an extended wheelbase of 13 ft. 11 ins., thus enabling a 26-seat body to be fitted. Prior to this specifically p.s.v. chassis entering the scene a few WTL lorry chassis had been modified for this purpose. One such WTL was CEV 394 which had a Motts 25-seat front entrance coach body fitted, and another Essex registered coach (DTW 215) had one that also sat 25 passengers. The WTB began to interest some of the 'big boys', which had not been the case with the WHB and the WLB. In 1935 Bristol Tramways bought one (No. 892, WV 3138) with a Duple body, following this up, in 1939, with an order for seven more (Nos. 200–6, FHT 817–23), also with Duple bodywork. By that late date a slightly more powerful version of the WTB had been produced with a 28 h.p. unit. In 1937 Devon General bought a pair of WTBs with Birch bus bodies seating 24 (Nos. 360/1, CTT 660/1) and another bus of this vintage went to Luton Corporation as their No. 60 (BBM 245). In the Metropolitan area City Coach Company purchased one bus WTB (B10, DXM 833) followed by a second in 1939 (B9, GVX 921). Silcox of Pembroke Dock started off, in 1938, with No. 7 (DDE 222), followed up next year with Nos. 3 (EDE 16) and 1 (DDE 963), the latter having a Thomas 25-seat body. But perhaps the place to really appreciate the WTB in that halcyon summer of 1939 was the 'Queen of the South' – Bournemouth. Here the Corporation ran them on such routes as No. 5 to Alum Chine past all the boarding houses among the pines, No. 19 along the Bourne Valley to the borough boundary, and No. 15 that linked the two piers as the Guy Runabouts and the S.D. Freighters had done at an earlier period. The 1937 batches (Nos. 174–6, DEL 657–9 and 177–80,

DLJ 38–41) had Duple bodies, as had the first two of the 1938 group (Nos. 181/2, EEL 43/4); the rest of the 1938 vehicles (Nos. 1–12, EEL 45–56) and those which came in 1939 (Nos. 13–16, FEL 216–9) had Burlingham bodywork (from the 'Queen of the North'!). Fortunately, two of the last quartet have been preserved for us still to enjoy their graceful lines with all the promise of days of sunshine. Each of them sat 25. A total of 2,556 WTBs were sold in Britain plus a further 664 overseas.

In 1938 Devon General requested Birch Bros. to fit 14-seat bus bodies to a pair of lorry designed Bedford WLG chassis for their Nos. M418/9 (EUO 192/3).

## Bedford OWB. Pl. 84, 85

The month before the Second World War began Bedfords stopped assembling the WTB and began to produce a newer form, known as the OB. The next few weeks saw the need for excursion coaches and promenade buses vanish for the next six years, so that of the pre-war OBs, only 73 were ever manufactured (52 of them being bought on the home market). Although we usually associate the number 29 with the seats of the OB, in fact the pre-war vehicles normally sat only 26. The wheelbase of the WTB had been lengthened to 14 ft. 6 ins., but the normal control and the WTB's 1938 vintage 28 h.p. engine were retained in the OB.

As from January 1942 operators who were near the top of the priority queue could buy a wartime version of the OB, namely the OWB. The 3,189 OWB chassis which came into their hands between that date and September 1945, received a wide variety of 32-seat utility bodies, normally with wooden slat seats. A standard wide bus-type indicator box was provided at the front. Most operators tried to replace these comparative 'eyesores' with post-war OBs as soon as

possible, but some had a long run for their money, as witness those operated by Portsmouth Corporation (Nos. 161–70), a number of which ended their days still transporting people for other departments of the city council, and one which escaped to be preserved. The Isle of Man Road Services were still operating their OWBs on specially scheduled journeys as late as 1966.

Bournemouth Corporation continued their series with Nos. 183–5 (FRU 101–3) in 1942 and Nos. 186–8 (FRU 104–6) the following year. The latter had Mulliner 29-seat bodies; this was a make that founds its way into several big fleets (Portsmouth 162/3 for example). North of the border, Highland Omnibuses had as many as three body builders for a sequence of only seven vehicles (Nos. 12–18: Duple, S.M.T., Highland). Even Edinburgh Corporation found it necessary to buy some OWBs (Nos. X1–10/16–25). Across the Irish Sea the Lough Swilly & Londonderry Railway bought a pair of OWBs in 1943 (Nos. 24/5, UI 3827/8). Though nearly all OWBs had front entrances, Exeter Corporation did have six with 32-seat rear entrance Duple bodies. (Nos. 71–6, FFJ 967–72).

In 1945 City Coach Company bought a modified OWLD lorry chassis for a brace of 20-seater buses (Nos. B14/5, JVX 943/4).

## Bristol 4 Ton

In 1920 Bristol introduced their Four Tonner designed to carry a 29-seat single-deck body. This had a 4 cylinder engine of the L headed type, with a bore of $4\frac{1}{2}$ ins. and a stroke of $5\frac{3}{4}$ ins., which developed 40 b.h.p. at 1,400 r.p.m. Transmission was through a single plate dry clutch and a 4 speed gearbox. The wheelbase was 14 ft. 6 ins.

Doncaster Corporation patronised this model, and had 30-seat dual entrance/exit bodies fitted to Nos. 1–6 (WY 5608–10/5734–6) in 1922. Further batches arrived in 1923 (Nos. 7–9), 1924 (Nos. 10–13) and 1925 (Nos. 17–20). Note that before 1927, Doncaster used West Riding registrations. J.M.T. bought seven 4 Tonners in 1923 as their Nos. 1–7. These had bodies similar to the Doncaster vehicles. By the 1925 Olympia this Bristol GW engine had improved to 52 b.h.p. at 1,000 r.p.m. and to 75 b.h.p. at 2,000 r.p.m.

At this date the chassis was redesigned to meet the demands for a low line. Also with a slight lengthening of the wheel-base to 15 ft. 7 ins. it was possible to fit 32-seat bodies, of overall length 24 ft. 9 ins. and of 7 ft. width. By the following Commercial Motor Show this model had been christened the Superbus and it appeared in two guises. The EB was designed to take a dual entrance/exit body, and the CB just a front entrance. It became the famous Bristol B series which found favour with many operators. For example, Exeter Corporation tried out a pair in 1929; Nos. 3/4 (FJ 6152/3) with their Northern Counties bodywork were of the EB variety. On the other hand Doncaster's very first registration was issued to a CB (No. 24, DT 1) with a Roe body. Rhondda had batches in 1927 (Nos. 47–9) and 1928 (Nos. 51–5) with Bristol's own B.B.W. bodies only this time they had rear entrances. Bristol Tramways themselves, the proprietors of Bristol Commercial Vehicles, invested in a good number of the GW engined B model, Nos. 337–593 and 657–60 arriving between 1929 and 1933.

## Bristol JO5G. Pl. 12, 86

The single-deck counterpart of the Bristol GO5G was the JO5G and it was powered by the same Gardner 5 cylinder oil unit. Bristol Tramways themselves started taking the JO5G into their fleet as early as 1933 and some sequences were quite long (e.g. Nos. 2000–80). Eastern National, another member of the Tilling group, had a mixture of 31-seat bus and dual purpose bodies fitted, with either front or rear entrances, to their 1936–7 JO5Gs (Nos. 3615–33/66–85/3714–37). Outside this group, Black & White Motorways decided to try out one batch of JOs with 31-seat Burlingham coach bodies (Nos. 78–85, BAD 631–8), and a second with Eastern Coachworks 30-seat coach bodies (Nos. 86–93, CDD 1–6/ 8–11). Because they needed more power for some of their express coaches, Black & White took the rarer JO6G version with the Gardner 6LW unit.

In 1937 Bristol Tramways had six of their JOs fitted with A.E.C. 7.7 litre engines and Nos. 2201–6 (DHY 653–8) were therefore classified as JO6As. On the other hand, in that year another new lot of JOs in the Bristol Tramway ranks had the smaller Dennis O4 engines fitted and are usually referred to as JO4Gs (Nos. 1240–5).

## Bristol L5G. Pl. 90

A natural successor to the JO series was the L series of single-deck chassis. Most of them were fitted with the Gardner 5LW oil engine and are therefore called L5Gs. Bristol Tramways used them mainly on their country routes although C2705–10 were bought for the city routes, in Bristol itself. Among non-Tilling buyers were Maidstone & District who purchased a trio of L5Gs in 1941 (Nos. SO 1–3, GKR 611–3).

Black & White Motorways continued to patronise Bristols and followed up their JO6Gs with batches of L6Gs (e.g. Nos. 100–5, DDF 44–9 with Duple 31-seat coach bodywork, in 1939). However, Bristol Tramways itself, employed some L4Gs with Gardner 4LW engines for their Gloucester area services (Nos. 1246–58, CFH 19–25/603–8).

The Maidstone & District L5Gs mentioned above were some of the 15 'unfrozen' L5Gs released by the Ministry of Supply in 1941–2, to needy operators. Three went to Scotland, entering the

I

ranks of Caledonian (Nos. 275/6, FSM 380/1) and Edinburgh Corporation (No. X15, DSF 987). Thereafter, production of the L5G ceased until 1946.

## Bristol A Type

At the 1925 Commercial Motor Show Bristol displayed the double-deck version of their new low line B or Superbus, called the A. It had a wheelbase of 16 ft. and was designed to take a 60-seat body. As often happened in those days, in reality, the production models often carried less than the prototype. Thus Doncaster Corporation placed into service in 1926, two A type Bristols (Nos. 55/6, WU 9230/1) with 52-seat open staircase bodies built by Short Bros. A third A followed two years later as No. 57 (DT 750).

## Bristol GO5G

From 1932 until 1937 Bristol produced their GO5G double-decker powered by a 5 cylinder Gardner oil engine. Bristol Tramways themselves used many for their services within that city (i.e. C3000–3081), as well as five on country routes (1515–9). Brighton, Hove & District following brief 'flirt' with the Dennis Lance after its long association with the A.E.C. Regent turned to the GO5G in 1936, when they took two batches with Eastern Counties 56-seat bodies (Nos. 6318–22, NJ 8718–22 and 6323–27, NJ 9056–60). Two trios of these buses followed in Coronation Year, namely Nos. 6328–30 (AAP 828–30) and 6331–3 (ANJ 831–3). Exeter Corporation also bought some GO5Gs in 1935, and Nos. 45–8 (BFJ 155–8) had 52-seat Bristol bodywork.

## Bristol K5G. Pl. 87–89

Writing in *British Double Deckers Since 1942* (p. 30) Alan Townsin remarks that: 'Always regarded as an "engineer's bus", it was intended primarily to meet the operating requirements of the Tilling group of operators. Eastern Coachworks, like the Bristol concern, a member of the Tilling group, built standardised body-work for the model.'

Thus in 1937 the K5G was launched on its very successful career as successor to the GO5G. As in this earlier model, it was powered by the Gardner 5LW engine. Some of the Tilling group (e.g. Brighton, Hove & District) wanted the highbridge 56-seat form, others wanted the alternative lowbridge version. For example, United Counties began their K5G series in 1938 with Nos. 477–84 (NV 9817/8 and VV 6347–52) which had 55-seat bodies, whereas Wilts & Dorset's Nos. 188–99 (CHR 487–98) of 1940, had only 52-seat bodies.

The K5G also found favour outside the Tilling group. Maidstone & District bought twelve in 1938 fitted with 48-seat lowbridge Weymann bodies (Nos. 270–81, FKL 601–12) and their subsidiary, Chatham & District, received four more of the same type (Nos. 352–5, FKL 613–6). The latter also had many, but with 54-seat highbridge Weymann bodies, delivered the following year as their Nos. 870–906 (GKE 64–100). Luton Corporation tried out a K5G (DTM 75) with a 55-seater Duple body in 1942 which leads us on to the introduction of so-called 'unfrozen' K5G buses into many fleets which would not, formerly, buy Bristol vehicles. For, of the 841 K5Gs built between 1937 and 1942, 85 of these came into this category. Some went of course, to Tilling group members (e.g. Hants & Dorset received TD 768–71), but others ended up with a variety of operators such as Derby Corporation (No. 74, RC 8274) and Moore of Kelvedon (JPU 640).

In 1944 the K chassis appeared, with the A.E.C. 7·7 litre diesel unit, as the K6A. Luton took four (Nos. 84–7, DMJ 84–7) with Park Royal 56-seat bodies of utility format and Maidstone & District swamped their fleet with K6As during 1944–5. Nos. DH 100–42 (HKE 201–43) and DH 143–9 (HKE 851–7) had Park Royal 56-seat bodies, DH 150–62 (HKE 858–70) had similar Duple bodies. Altogether 251 K6As were built.

## Chevrolet LM. Pl. 91, 92

Chevrolets, during the 1920s and early 1930s, brought out a whole, and rather confusing, range of chassis designed to carry 14-seat bodies. The following table of approximate dates may help the reader:

| Model | Years |
|---|---|
| 2A | 1923 |
| B | 1924–5 |
| X | 1926–7 |
| LM | 1927 |
| LO/LP | 1928 |
| LQ/LR/LZ | 1929 |
| U | 1930 |

The LM, as it appeared at the 1927 Commercial Motor Show, was a 25-cwt. chassis incorporating a 4 cylinder engine with a bore/stroke of $3\frac{11}{16}$ in./4 in. and a wheelbase of only 10 ft. 4 ins. However, an advertisement of that time called upon Chevrolet LM owners to bring their chassis and to have them converted into 6-wheelers for the additional sum of only £96. This would add 50 per cent. in carrying capacity, and it is what Gosport & Fareham did with their LOs, LPs, LQs and LRs during 1928–30. Thus LP No. 1 (OU 224) became a 20-seater bus and LQ No. 17 (OU 3713) sat as many as 26 after this transformation! Nevertheless others preferred to retain their originally planned 14-seat bodies. For instance Safeguard of Guildford in 1930 kept their HX 320, HX 482 and HX 3084.

## Commer 3P. Pl. 13

At the 1921 Commercial Motor Show Commers showed their 3P chassis which was suitable for larger single-deckers and for double-deckers. It was powered by a 40 h.p. 4 cylinder engine with bore/stroke of 120 mm/140 mm. Transmission was in the form of a Thomas 4 speed gearbox, the final drive being by over-type worm working in a phosphor-bronze wheel. The wheelbase was 15 ft. 10 ins. Glasgow Corporation bought a pair of 3P buses in 1924, Nos. 1/2 (GB 6900/1) were given Norfolk 30-seat dual entrance/exit bodies. There was a smaller chassis known as the 2P in the early 'twenties.

At the 1927 Show the above two were partially replaced by the F4 and the N4; they were forward and normal control versions of the same chassis which had a wheelbase of 16 ft. 4 ins. The power unit was a 4 cylinder petrol engine with a bore of 110 mm and a stroke of 140 mm which developed 82 b.h.p. at 2,500 r.p.m. The brakes had Dewandre servo assistance and the final drive was by means of underneath worm drive. The N4 could seat 26 and the F4 32. In 1928 there appeared 6 cylinder versions of these two models, called the N6 and F6, which a year later were superseded by the 4PN and 4PF models.

## Commer Avenger

When the Commer NF6 made its debut in 1930 it was advertised as either a 32-seat single-deck bus or as a 50-seat double-decker. As it happened only the former version was in fact, built, This was a forward control bus and it remained the heaviest Commer p.s.v. chassis in production during the decade leading up to the Second World War. UN 5382 is an example of an Avenger with a 30-seat forward entrance bus body. A 6 cylinder petrol engine was provided with this model.

After the cessation of the Avenger's production in 1934, a gap of five years intervened, before another 32-seater emerged from the Commer stable. This was the 'Superpoise', rather surprisingly a normal control model unlike the NF6.

In 1942 Mansfield & District bought two Superpoise tractors powered by Perkins P6 engines, to pull Weyman 38-seat trailers.

## Commer PNF Series. Pl. 93

Between 1936–9 Commer introduced a range of smaller coach chassis, powered by a series of 6 cylinder petrol engines, which increased in its seating capacity. In the case of the PLNF5 there existed an option on a 6 cylinder Perkins diesel unit. This model was also three inches wider than the equivalent PN4. These forward control models are best presented in tabular form:

| Model | Years | Seats |
|-------|-------|-------|
| PNF3 | 1936–7 | 20 |
| PN4 | 1936–7 | 20 |
| PNF4 | 1936–7 | 26 |
| PLN5 | 1938–9 | 20 |
| PLNF5 | 1938–9 | 26 |

Baddeley Bros. patronised the Commer PN3 for Waveney-bodied coaches registered as BWR 685, BWY 724 and CWW 109. AAW 32 had a rare Rees & Griffiths bus body, and another rare body could be found on YJ 3667, a PNF4 with a Cadogan 26-seat coach body. DDH 343 was a PLNF5 with a fully-fronted 27-seat coach body.

## Commer Invader

During 1930 Commer introduced their small control 6TK model, known as the Invader. It could take either a 14- or a 20-seat body. Exeter Corporation purchased one as their No. 15 (FJ 7069) which had a Willowbrook 20-seat bus body fitted. Another example of it as a small bus could be found in the ranks of Rover Bus Services of Buckinghamshire with their KX 6691, which possessed a 20-seat Petty body.

A similar chassis of this period but with altered frontal design was the Centaur, named after the 'parent' of Commer Cars of Luton. Some Centaurs had 20-seat bodies (e.g. JH 2340 with one by Thurgood and EV 9529 with one by Duple), while other Centaurs had more again. For instance AWU 562, of 1935 vintage, had a 24-seat body, while Baddeley Brothers' No. 18 (YG 9795) of 1934 went one better. A special luxury version of the Centaur was known as the Centurion, but it was very rarely built.

A lengthened form of the Invader, built during 1931–3, was named the Corinthian. This normal control model was designed to seat 26 passengers as did UJ 425, and which was used as a bus. On the other hand JC 690 sat only 24 people.

A forward control version of the Centaur, the Greyhound, which sat 26, appeared in 1934. A year later the B3 emerged, and this was merely a variant of the Greyhound. Hanford's BRE 320 was an example of this and it had a fully-fronted coach body fitted.

## Crossley Eagle

The first chassis, specifically designed for p.s.v. work, that came from the Crossley Works was the Eagle, which was launched in 1928. This was a single-deck model with a 4 cylinder Crossley 30/70 engine (i.e. 30 h.p., developing 70 b.h.p.). With a capacity of 5·3 litres this petrol unit had a bore of $4\frac{5}{16}$ in. and a stroke of $5\frac{1}{2}$ in. As seen in other instances in the 'twenties, this engine had been evolved from that supplied for the larger private cars built by the manufacturer. It had a dry plate clutch and a 4 speed sliding mesh gearbox, mounted amidships. Single vacuum servo brakes were fitted and the final drive was through underslung worm to the rear axle. The wheelbase was 16 ft. $7\frac{1}{2}$ ins., and it was planned that a 28-seat bus body should be carried. The model was a forward control one. Among the 74 Eagles sold were two, supplied to Norfolk Motor Services, who had 32-seat Eaton bodies built for their Nos. 1/2 (EX 2360/89). Leeds Corporation were another customer having Roe rear entrance bus bodies fitted to vehicles such as No. 75 (UA 5825). The last Eagle appeared in 1932.

In 1929 a 6 cylinder version of the Eagle went into production, and it was called the Arrow. The 6·8 litre engine had a 4 in. bore and a 5½ in. stroke, and the 38 h.p. unit developed 110 b.h.p. Perhaps because Dennis Bros. had also chosen the name Arrow for one of their single-deck designs, Crossleys changed to Alpha shortly afterwards. Indeed, whereas Aberdeen's Nos. 97–103 (RG 2210-6) with their 26-seat front entrance Cowieson bodywork were called Arrows, Edinburgh's SC 9901 with its 31-seat Alexanders dual entrance/exit body, was referred to as an Alpha—all very confusing! Norfolk Motor Services also purchased a pair of Alphas, again with 32-seat Eaton bodywork (Nos. 14/5, EX 2684/65). Ashton-under-Lyne's duo of Alphas (Nos. 21/2, ATC 975/6), of 1935 vintage, had 32-seat M.C.W. bodies. A later one (No. 32, CTD 788) had a Crossley body.

In 1937 the Alpha was redesigned and given a new measurement for its wheelbase, 17 ft. 7 ins. Manchester Corporation took 20 of these single-deck buses which also had Crossley semi-streamlined bodies. The final pair of Alphas went to Sunderland Corporation in 1939 and were given locally built Blagg bodies. Incidentally, after the Second World War this municipality bought other Alphas – underfloor chassis built by Atkinsons!

**Crossley Condor.** Pl. 15, 16
In 1930 Crossleys introduced their first double-decker, the Condor. This had the same 6 cylinder engine as the Arrow/ Alpha, though very shortly afterwards Leeds Corporation made history by placing on service the first diesel engined double-decker – a Condor powered by a Gardner 6L2 engine, originally made for so-called 'light' marine work. This was a 8·4 litre unit with bore/stroke of 4¼ in./ 6 in. A second 6L2 engined Condor went to Sheffield Corporation. By the end of 1932, Crossleys with oil engines, totalled 158, which were more than even A.E.C. could claim at that time. Manchester Corporation headed the list with 64 Condors in service, and Portsmouth were in second place. The latter, having tried out No. 74 (RV 746) in 1931, with a 48-seat Short Bros. body, ordered a further twenty for delivery the next year. Nos. 95–114 (RV 1990–2009) had 50-seat English Electric bodywork. Aberdeen Corporation decided to mix their Arrow with Condors, and took into stock Nos. 85–96 (RG 1790–1803) in 1931, followed by Nos. 9–16 (RG 3671–8) in 1933. All had 48- or 52-seat Walker bodies. Perth Corporation, in its last days of motorbus operation, tried out a brace of Condors with Pickering bodies seating only 46 passengers (Nos. 32/3, GS 3919/20). Leicester's No. 69 (JF 5000) was nick-named 'Buster' by its drivers. This had a Crossley-Ricardo VR6 engine of 8·365 litres, with a bore of 4$\frac{7}{16}$ in. and a stroke of 5½ in. Other Condors had appeared with a 9·12 litre Crossley-Ricardo engine and Gardner 6LW units.

The Condor was replaced by the Mancunian (in honour of Manchester, the home town of Crossleys) which had a wheelbase of 16 ft. 7½ ins. (the same as for the Condor). This time, however, the gearbox was positioned directly behind the engine, whereas the earlier model had had it amidships. As might have been expected, most of the Mancunians entered the fleet of Manchester Corporation, although a few did go as far afield as Maidstone Corporation and Stockton-on-Tees Corporation. Indeed the very last Mancunian built became No. 45 (GKK 984) in the Kent municipal fleet just after the outbreak of the Second World War. Ashton-under-Lyne Corporation took batches of Mancunians in

1934 (Nos. 2–4, TJ 5793–5), 1935 (Nos. 1/9, ATC 973/4), 1936 (Nos. 10–12/23–25, ATJ 891–6), 1937 (Nos. 26–8, BTJ 624–6) and 1938 (Nos. 33–6, DTE 321–4).

## Crossley TDD Series

Like Daimlers Crossley were one of the last manufacturers to take up the construction of trolleybuses. It was in 1936 that they built their prototype TDD6 (i.e. Trolleybus Double-Decker six-wheeler) which was given an M.C.W. 68-seat body and which entered the fleet of Ashton-under-Lyne as their No. 58 (CNE 474). It had a wheelbase of 18 ft. 7 ins. and possessed Kirkstall rear axles. The worm drive casing was centrally positioned instead of being offset. Metro-Vick 206 motors and electrical equipment were standard to both the TDD6 and the TDD4, the latter being the four-wheeled version. Two more TDD6s were supplied to Ashton-under-Lyne Corporation (Nos. 46/7, CTF 313/4) and later two others went to Belfast Corporation (Nos. 3/4, EZ 7891/2). However, the majority of this type built by Crossleys went to Manchester Corporation.

The first TDD4, with its reduced wheelbase of 16 ft., went also to Ashton-under-Lyne in 1936, becoming No. 49 (CTD 787). A further eight followed in 1940 (Nos. 50/1, 53/4, 56/7 and 59/60, ETE 811–8). Hull Corporation took delivery of more TDD4s in 1938 in the form of Nos. 27–45 (ERH 27–45), bearing 60-seat Craven bodies. However it was once again Manchester Corporation, who took the lion's share of the 97 TDD4s which came off the asembly lines until production stopped in 1940, when the Gorton chassis erection shops were destroyed during a blitz on Manchester, in December of that year.

## Daimler CK Series. Pl. 52

In 1919 Daimler added to their pre-war range of commercial chassis the CK, suitable, as were most chassis of that era, for either single-deck or double-deck bodywork. The CK had a wheelbase of 13 ft. 6 ins. and was powered by a 4 cylinder 22·4 h.p. engine, which developed 30 b.h.p. at 1,000 r.p.m. Its bore was 90 mm and its stroke 140 mm. With a 4 speed cone gearbox incorporated, the final drive came through Lanchester type worm gearing. The frame was constructed of flitch plate and wood. Although many operators persevered with the older Daimler Y chassis Birmingham Corporation did buy some of the CK2 version. Their No. 80 (OK 9852) in 1923 was fitted with a Strachan & Brown 19-seat body and a further batch (Nos. 81–88, OL 1714–21) had larger, 23-seat bodywork, by the same builder.

At the 1925 Olympia Show the CK presented an improved 5·1 litre engine with a bore of 104·5 mm and a stroke of 150 mm. This 4 cylinder unit had an R.A.C. rating of 36 h.p. and developed 45 b.h.p. at 1,500 r.p.m. In other respects it remained similar to the earlier model. However two longer versions of the CK were also shown in 1925. The CL had a wheelbase of 15 ft. 6 ins. and the CM's measurement was up to 16 ft., which enabled a 36-seat single-decker body to be fitted, since the overall length of the chassis was 24 ft. 4 ins. The chassis was still the old fashioned straight type and solid tyres were fitted. Trent put into service one of the first CM buses, their No. 810 (CH 4856) which had a Ransomes 31-seat body with front entrance.

During 1927–8 the A.D.C. 423 and 424 replaced the CK, CL and CM. The 423 was a forward control single-decker with a wheelbase of 16 ft. 3½ ins. It was powered by a Daimler engine of 3·57 litres with a bore of 81·5 mm and a stroke of 114 mm, as had been the former A.D.C. 416D and 417D models which had had A.E.C. chassis. The 424 was a normal control single-decker with a wheelbase of 17 ft. 3⅞ ins. and it was powered by the same unit as used in the 423. Edinburgh took into the fleet eight of the A.D.C. 423 (SC 1130–37) which bore 32-seat dual entrance/exit Croall bodies; examples of the 424 could be found in the ranks of Royal Blue of Bournemouth (RU 6711–36).

In 1929–30 the former A.D.C. 423 and 424 were replaced by the Daimler CF6, the numeral standing for its improved 6 cylinder engine. This had a capacity of 5·76 litres, a bore of 97 mm and a stroke of 130 mm. Its sleeve-valves enabled a much higher compression ratio to be achieved than in the earlier poppet-valve units. The CF6 was available in both the wheelbase dimension of the 423 and that of the 424. Edinburgh bought batches of the CF6 fitted with 32- or 31-seat dual entrace/exit bodies in 1929 (SC 3416, Croall bodywork), 1930 (SC 7285–320, Cowieson bodywork) and 1931 (SC 9904–17, Alexanders Motors bodywork). Likewise, Elliotts of Bournemouth (alias Royal Blue), continued their patronage with LJ 652 in 1929 and LJ 1501–9/29–33 in the following year. Among smaller operators, Burwell & District in Cambridgeshire, purchased four CF6s as their Nos. 5 (MT 3957), 6 (ER 9437), 7 (VE 1050) and 9 (VE 5551).

## Daimler CG6 Series

By 1931 the old straight chassis frame was out of date and so Daimler replaced their CF6 with a new CG6. Although keeping the 6 cylinder engine, gearbox and single-plate clutch of the CF6, the CG6 had a much lower frame. Since normal control vehicles of a larger size were no longer in great demand only forward control models of the CG6 were built.

The CG6 was soon replaced by the CH6 which had the same engine as its predecessor but incorporated a new Daimler fluid flywheel and Wilson self-changing gearbox. Luton Corporation bought several of the CH6 for both single-deck and double-deck duties. Nos. 1–5 (TM 9876–80) of 1932 vintage had Duple 32-seat rear entrance bus bodies and Nos. 15–17 (MJ 1031 and 1587/8) had 28-seat Willowbrook bodies. All the double-deckers had 52-seat lowbridge type bodies, by either Duple (Nos. 6–9, TM 9881–84; 10–12, MJ 183–5; 13/4, MJ 434/3) or Willowbrook (Nos. 18/9, MJ 1589/90; 29/30, MJ 2336/7; 31–3, MJ 2747–9; 34/5, MJ 2879/80; 36/7, MJ 4151/2). Edinburgh continued his series with FS 2159–67 which carried 30-seat Cowieson bodies. Among independent operators, Ledgard purchased UG 7252, a CH6 with a 54-seat highbridge body built by Roberts. Walsall Corporation's No. 100 (DH 8638) had a rare 54-seat body by Buckingham of Birmingham.

The successor of the CH6 was the CP6 which introduced a new 6 cylinder engine of 6·56 litres with bore/stroke dimensions of 103·5 mm and 130 mm respectively. Although the letters following C for Commercial in Daimler p.s.v. designations are usually without significance, in the case of CP6, the P stood for Poppet, for this type of valve had replaced the sleeve valve used on the CH6 and previous models. The CP6 found favour with several large municipalities including Coventry, its city of origin, whose Nos. 101–16 (KV 7101–16) had 50-seat Brush bodies and were followed, later in 1934, by a similar batch numbered 120–22 (KV 9210–2). Doncaster fitted 52-seat Roe bodywork to their pair of CP6s, Nos. 62/4 (DT 3692 and DT 4149) and Birmingham returned to the Daimler fold with a small consignment consisting of Nos. 554–63 (OC 554–63) which had 51-seat B.R.C.W.C. bodies. Dundee (Nos. 30/2, TS 9111/2), were among those who used the CP6 with a single-deck body – in this case a dual entrance/exit one by Dickson, seating 31 passengers.

## Daimler COG Series. Pl. 94, 95

Perhaps one of the greatest of Daimler's successes during the period between the two wars was achieved with their COG5-DD which made its debut in 1934. This was basically the CF6 but with a diesel engine. Its designation was deliberate and meant Commercial Oil Gardner 5-cylinder Double-Decker. The Gardner engine involved was the increasingly popular 5LW with its capcaity of 7·00 litres, bore of 4½ in. and a stroke of 6 in. Between 1934 and 1939 Birmingham took delivery of a steady stream of COG5-DDs starting with No. 566 (AOB 566) which had a 50-seat B.R.C.W.C. body, down to No. 1269 (FOF 269) which had a 54-seat B.R.C.W.C. body. During this period the total intake numbered some 694 buses.

Some operators, however, liked a more powerful form of the COG5-DD, the COG6-DD. This had as its engine the 8·40 litre Gardner 6LW, with a bore of 4¼ in. and a stroke of 6 in. Dundee Corporation liked this model and purchased three separate batches, Nos. 154-7 (YJ 4115/6/20/1) in 1936, Nos. 104-11 (YJ 7055-62) in 1939 and Nos. 96-103 (YJ 7047-54) in 1940. Another Scottish burgh with interest in the COG6-DD was Glasgow in 1937, Nos. 510-34 (BGA 76-100) had 56-seat Weyman bodies.

Coventry preferred the A.E.C. engined COA6-DD. This was powered by the 7·7 litre unit with a bore of 105 mm and a stroke of 146 mm. Between 1934 and 1939 Coventry took into its ranks no less than eight different batches of COA6-DDs with a variety of bodies built by Brush, Massey and M.C.W.

A single-deck version called the COG5-SD was offered for sale from 1933 until 1936. Normally this had seats for 36 passengers. During the 1930s the famous sloping line of the Daimler radiator became popular but it was decided in 1936 to make the radiator of the single-decker vertical, thus enabling the bulkhead to be moved forward and another four passengers to be seated. Consequently it was named the COG5-40. Luton Corporation had 39-seat Willowbrook bodies fitted and Coventry's Park Royal bodied COG5-40s seated 38. On the other hand P.M.T. bought COG5-40s that only sat 35, with bodies by either Weyman or English Electric. A double-deck version of the COG5-40, called the COG5-60, was built in 1939-40 especially for Coventry Corporation. The Brush bodies seated 60. A COG6-40 was built but its long wheelbase of 18 ft. 9 ins. made it unacceptable under traffic regulations then in force and it was manufactured by Daimler purely for export.

## Daimler CTM

One of the late entrants into trolleybus manufacturing was Daimler. Only in 1936 did they announce the appearance of their CTM range. The initials stood for Commercial Trolleybus Metro-Vick, the latter being the makers of the motors and electrical equipment fitted into the Daimler trolleybuses. This was rather unusual although at one time Karrier did work a similar scheme with Cloughs. The 'range' consisted of two models, the six-wheel CTM6 and the four-wheel CTM4.

Only three CTM6s were produced before work ceased at the onset of the Second World War. Two of these went to Belfast Corporation as Nos. 5/6 (EZ 7893/4). Newcastle-upon-Tyne Corporation were the recipients of the third CTM6 which became No. 112 (DHP 112) in their fleet. The Coventry registration suggests that it was used as a demonstrator by Daimler before proceeding north for the rest of its working life. The 60-seat dual entrance/exit body was by M.C.W.

The CTM4 was relatively successful

compared with its bigger brother. Fourteen were sold to West Hartlepool Corporation, six to Derby Corporation and one to South Shields (No. 234, CWK 67). Daimler did not resume their role as trolleybus manufacturers until 1950 when the CTM4 and the CTM6 again appeared in the catalogues emanating from Coventry.

## Daimler CW Series. Pl. 96–98

After a pause of two years the government permitted Daimler to recommence manufacturing bus chassis at the beginning of 1943. The resulting product was the CW series (in this case W stood for Wartime), starting with the CWG5, which was in reality the pre-war COG5 but with certain aluminium parts replaced by steel or cast iron ones. In place of the former Daimler rear axle one made by Kirkstall was substituted. Birmingham took delivery of three CWG5s as their Nos. 1338–40 (FOP 338–40), fitted with Utility style 56-seat highbridge bodies built by Duple. A similar pair went to Maidstone & District as their Nos. DH 30/1 (GKN 268/9). All Daimler patrons, such as Aberdeen, received CWGs (Nos. 136/7, BRG 838/9). Other operators had to take Daimler for the first time, for instance Wilts & Dorset with their Nos. 260–3 (CWV 778–81) fitted with Brush lowbridge 55-seat bodies. A few CWG6s were built with the Gardner 6LW engine. Two of these went to Devon General as Nos. DD 241/2 (HTA 881/2).

In September 1943 a second type, the CWA6, appeared on the scene. This was the wartime equivalent to the COA6 with the same 7·7 litre A.E.C. unit. Birmingham took some fifty-five of this variety and had to take at the same time a motley collection of bodies from the workshops of Brush, Duple and Park Royal. Brush, Duple, Massey and Northern Counties were responsible for the bodies on the CWA6s sent to Dundee Corporation

during the period 1943–45 as their Nos. 80–95. Glasgow at this time also chose thirty-two CWA6s as replacement double-deckers. London Transport started their new D class in 1944 and it eventually contained 168 CWA6s with either Brush or Duple bodies. Smaller municipal fleets that had perforce to welcome in the CWA6 included Exeter (Nos. 77–83, GFJ 48–54), Doncaster (Nos. 87–89, CDT 309–11) and Portsmouth (Nos. 171–79). Ledgard built up their fleet by adding four with Roe bodywork (JUA 915–18) and eight with Duple bodywork (JUB 128/9 and JUB 649–52/8/9). Altogether about 1,260 CWAs were built.

Early in 1945 Daimlers were allowed to install their own 8·60 litre engine which had been designed as long ago as 1939. This 6 cylinder engine had a bore of $4\frac{1}{2}$ in. and a stroke of $5\frac{1}{2}$ in. Of the one hundred CWD6s produced London Transport received thirteen (D 127/38–40/42/50/5/60/2/3/71/80/1), Glasgow five (Nos. 154–58, DUS 460–64), Birmingham seven (Nos. 1420–25, FOP 420–25 and 1480, FOP 480), and Ledgard two (JUB 647/8). The CWD6s had Daimler rear axles, as had the final one hundred CWA6s, which are sometimes referred to as CWA6Ds.

## Dennis 30-cwt. Pl. 100–103

At the 1925 Commercial Motor Show Dennis displayed their neat little normal control 30-cwt., sometimes called the Chaser. Its 4 cylinder Dennis engine developed 36 b.h.p. at 2,000 r.p.m. with a bore of 85 mm and a stroke of 120 mm. Having a wheelbase of 11 ft. the overall length of the chassis was only 15 ft. 7 ins. It was certainly a low load line vehicle and its rear axle stood a mere $10\frac{5}{8}$ ins. off the road surface.

During 1927–8 the 30-cwt. found favour with several of the larger operators including Southdown, who ordered twenty. Nos. 501–18 (UF 1501–18) bore front entrance 19-seat bodies built by

Shorts and Harringtons of Hove supplied the bodywork for the remaining two: 519 (UF 1519) was an 18-seater coach and 520 (UF 1520) a 19-seater bus. Wilts & Dorset purchased four small batches of 30-cwts. fitted with either 19- or 18-seat Short Bros. bodywork (Nos. 36–40/43–6).

At the 1927 Show Dennis Bros. decided that, in future, the 30-cwt. should be restricted to other commercial uses and for bus and coach work they substituted their model G. This was a slightly longer vehicle with a wheelbase of up to 11 ft. 10 ins. and an overall chassis length of 18 ft. 6¾ ins. The power unit remained unchanged but Dewandre servo-operated brakes were provided as an improvement. Both Southdown (Nos. 532, UF 4532) and Wilts & Dorset (No. 47, MW 1854) tried only one of the new G but Colchester Corporation bought four of them (Nos. 1–4, VW 4389–92) with Strachan & Brown 20-seat bus bodies; Edinburgh tried out three with Vickers bodywork (Nos. 501–3, SC 6028–30) and three with Croall bodywork (SC 1146–48). These last six were given 14-seat charabanc style bodies for city tours. National also bought one as a 14-seater coach (No. 2901, VX 249).

Perhaps the most remarkable trio of preserved vehicles from the year 1929 are the Dennis GL buses from Llandudno U.D.C. (CC 8694/9305/9424) with their canvas roof toastrack bodies by Roberts, each seating 19 passengers. This improved version of the G also found its way into the fleet of Potters Coaches of Wickford. VX 5364, VX 6863 and VX 9516 had 20-seat Duple bus bodies. The GL maintained the 30-cwt. chassis weight of its two predecessors.

The Dart was a 6 cylinder version of the GL but resembled that model in size and in normal control. Not many Darts entered the major fleets. Thomas Tilling did use four at Brighton in 1932 (Nos. 6251–4, GT 2251–4), made with com-

pany built 20-seat front entrance bodies, and designed for one man duties. Mexborough and Swinton commissioned London Lorries to build the bodywork for their 1933 vintage Darts (Nos. 1/2, YG 2478/9).

**Dennis Ace.** Pl. 104, 105
Introduced in 1934 was a small replacement for the Dennis GL and Dart, the Ace, a normal control vehicle with a new frame and new 4 cylinder engine. The Ace's special feature was its front axle which, placed to the rear of the bonnet, provided a very small turning circle needed on some rural routes. Because of its appearance the Ace earned the nickname 'Flying Pig'! A wide variety of operators found the Ace an answer to some of their problems. Thomas Tilling bought a pair (6306/7, NJ 4627/8) with Eastern Counties bodywork to run on two widely separated 'rural' services in the Brighton area, namely between Portslade Station and Mile Oak (route 9) in the west and betwixt Rottingdean and Woodingdean (route 2A) in the east. Southern Vectis found such vehicles as 405 (DL 9015), with its Harrington body, useful on the local 15/15A routes at Newport in the Isle of Wight. Over in Ireland G.N.R. fitted their own bodies to Nos. 33–5 (ZA 3827–9) and 36/7 (ZA 7154/5). Eastern National purchased twenty equipped with Dennis bodywork (Nos. 3595–614, CTW 191–210) and East Kent built their own bodies for a first batch in 1934 (JG 4225–50), but asked Park Royal to do this job for the second a year later (JG 5449–51).

Contemporary with the normal control Ace was the much less popular forward control Mace. In the Chilterns the Penn Bus Company, having bought an Ace as their No. 31 (APP 273), followed this up with No. 32 (BBH 755), a Mace. The main difference was that whereas the Ace sat 20 passengers, the other model had six additional seats. Few large concerns bought Maces but Bristol Tramways Company did invest in half a dozen with Duple bodywork in 1937 (Nos. 651-6, DHY 647-52). Some Maces had front entrances (as in the case of the Bristol vehicles) and others had a centrally positioned entrance (as with the Penn bus).

In 1936 a slightly larger version of the Ace entered the market entitled the Arrow Minor but few were sold. One (AET 456), having started off with Greaves of Rotherham, ended up in 1941 in the fleet of Silcox of Pembroke Dock as their No. 17. Its front entrance body seated 25 as did Harper Bros. No. 11 (GRE 167) carrying a Burlingham body. Twenty-six passengers, as in the case of CRA 72, seems to have been the maximum for the Arrow Minor.

The next stage in the development of the Ace was the Pike, built between 1938-40. Like the Arrow Minor the front axle had been moved to a more orthodox forward position. Again, few were constructed. One did find its way into the fleet of an active Guildford based operator, Yellow Bus Service, (GPF 117). This had a Dennis 20-seat front entrance body.

The Mace's successor was the Falcon which could seat 30 passengers as shown by Southdown's 80/1 (FUF 180/1) carrying Dennis bodies. However GAT 226 had a 31-seat Barnaby body while EF 7140 used one by Duple containing 32 seats. Guernsey Railway Company took some of these Falcons fitted with Dennis bodies (e.g. 3774). Although most pre-war Falcons were powered by Dennis petrol units a few were given small Perkins diesel engines.

## Dennis E. Pl. 99

Making its debut at the 1925 Show was the Dennis E type single-decker. This was a forward control model with a wheelbase of 16 ft., giving an overall body length of 25 ft. 0⅝ ins., and an improved width of 7 ft. 1 in. and thus enabling a 33-seat body to be fitted perfectly to the chassis. The E was given a new Dennis 4 cylinder engine developing 70 b.h.p. with a bore of 110 mm and a stroke of 150 mm.

Walsall Corporation was one of the first operators to see the advantage of this new low line vehicle, and during 1926, it placed into service Nos. 44-58 (DH 4905-9/5500-9) fitted with Vickers 31-seat rear entrance bodies. The following year a further batch arrived, this time with one additional seat provided (Nos. 61-8, DH 5902-9). In 1928 no less than twenty-nine additional Dennis E buses came to reside in this Staffordshire town, Nos. 69-97 (DH 6400-28). Portsmouth Corporation tried out an E in 1927 equipped with a 32-seat front entrance Ransomes body (No. 36, TP 4422) and decided to order a further eight E buses, but fitted with 32-seat rear entrance Davidsons bodywork (Nos. 54-61, TP 6864-71). J.M.T., in the Channel Islands, purchased three 32-seaters in 1929 (Nos. 29-31, J 5409-11). Of the West Bromwich quintet (Nos. 28-32, EA 4177-81), one with Dixon bodywork, has survived to demonstrate the solid and reliable lines of this Dennis product.

At the 1927 Show there appeared an improved version called the F. Powered by the same 4 cylinder engine as the E, its wheelbase had been lengthened to 16 ft. 7½ ins. The F seems to have appealed mainly to small coaching firms such as the Westminster Coaching Services who, during 1929-30, took delivery of four Fs, each seating 20 passengers in comfort (UL 5144/7, UL 7692 and GF 9510). Other F chassis came into service with 26-seat bodies, like EX 2065 and VX 610.

The 6 cylinder Dennis engine converted the E into the EV. During 1929-30 single-decker buses based on EV chassis appeared with 31- or 32-seat rear entrances (e.g. Portsmouth Nos. 62-7,

TP 8098–103), front entrances (e.g. Coventry No. 54, VC 6000) or even dual entrances/exits (e.g. Colchester Nos. 18/9, VX 2746/5).

**Dennis H.** Pl. 18

To replace their 4-ton double-decker of the period 1923-6 the Guildford firm of Dennis manufactured their H type as from 1927. Instead of being of normal control it was a forward control model on a wheelbase of 16 ft. 6¾ ins. and powered by the same 4 cylinder engine as the E type single-decker. Some of the first H buses built had open top bodies. Such were D146–8 (YW 8004–6) in the London General fleet and which were later renumbered DH1–3. Colchester Corporation's Nos. 10–12 (VW 6482/1 and VW 8425) similarly arrived roofless from Strachan & Brown during 1928–9 but later H buses coming into the fleet of that Essex town had top deck cover (e.g. Nos. 15–17, VX 3223/4/2). In comparison with the 48 seats on Colchester's Dennis H vehicles, Walsall specified 52 in their Short Bros. bodies, starting with Nos. 11–20 (DH 6300–9) in 1928.

West Bromwich Corporation took advantage of the more powerful 6 cylinder version called the HS (S for Six) in 1930 when they ordered their Nos. 36–8 (EA 4622–4) with Massey 50-seat lowbridge bodies.

A further improvement called the HV appeared during 1930–1. Like the HS it was powered by a Dennis 6 cylinder unit. Doncaster Corporation's Nos. 60/1 (DT 2114/5) had Roe 48-seat bodies fitted to their HV chassis.

**Dennis Lance.** Pl. 20

The Lance 1 was introduced by Dennis Bros. in 1931 as a 6 cylinder petrol engined double-deck chassis. The unit was a Dennis 6·1 litre engine with a bore of 100 mm and a stroke of 130 mm which developed 100 b.h.p. The radiator was

one which had been used previously in the Arrow. Walsall Corporation bought two batches with 54-seat Brush bodies in 1931 (Nos. 30–2, DH 8503–5 and 7–10, DH 8805–8) and one batch with 52-seat Beadle bodies (Nos. 33–7, DH 8506–10).

In 1933 the Lance 2 replaced the Lance 1 and it shared the same radiator design as the single-decker Lancet 2. Up to 1938 there was a choice between a petrol engine and a new 4 cylinder oil engine of 5·7 litres, with a bore of 110 mm, a stroke of 150 mm and developing 85 b.h.p. After 1938 only oil engined Lance 2 chassis were assembled. Walsall continued to take these Dennis double-deckers and Nos. 173–84 (EDH 301–12) in 1937 were fitted with Park Royal 52-seat bodies. Other clients of Dennis for the Lance over this period included Thomas Tilling who had their Brighton fleet (Nos. 6311–6, NJ 5974–9) fitted with the Company's own bodies, Coventry Corporation (Nos. 62/3, KV 724/5) with 50-seat Brush bodies and West Bromwich Corporation (Nos. 49–52, EA 6304–7). Nevertheless, it was home-based Aldershot & District who took the lions share of Lance 2s during the 'thirties.

During the short period 1936–7 a Lance 4 was produced. This used the new Dennis 'Big Four' petrol engine of 6·78 litres capacity, with a bore of 120 mm and a stroke of 150 mm. It was rated at 90 b.h.p. at 2,000 r.p.m. The alternative oil engine was slightly smaller with a capacity of 6·5 litres and a bore of 117·4 mm which led to a rating of 80 b.h.p. at 1,800 r.p.m. Once again a patron was found in Walsall who took twenty-five of these (Nos. 190–214, FDH 851–75) with Park Royal 54-seat bodies.

**English Electric Trolleybuses**

For a few years English Electric manufactured complete trolleybuses including chassis, bodies, motors and electrical equipment. Later on they concentrated on all but the first named function. Basically two versions were offered. There was the four-wheeler which was designed mainly for single-deck work and which was far more popular in the 'twenties than in the 'thirties. Notts & Derby Traction purchased six in 1932 (Nos. 300–5, RB 5568–73) fitted with 32-seat front entrance bodywork. Subsequently these were sold to Mexborough & Swinton for further service. Darlington Corporation tried out four such English Electric trolleybuses in 1926. Nos. 21–4 (HN 4770–3) had 31-seat central entrance bodywork and were powered by 60 h.p. motors. During the period 1928–30 they were followed into service by Nos. 27–32 (HN 6879–84) which had similar 32-seat bodies. Bradford Corporation had eleven single-deck four-wheelers in 1928 (Nos. 561–71, KW 6051–61).

The larger six-wheeled version was designed to receive double-decker bodies. Bradford became one of its chief patrons and took into its fleet two sets in 1929 (Nos. 572–7, KW 6062–7 and 578–83, KW 6654–9) and further trolleys of this type in 1930 (Nos. 584, KW 9433; 585–95, KW 9454–64 and 596, KY 1360). Maidstone Corporation was another client in 1929 (e.g. No. 24, KR 352).

**Ford T.** Pl. 106

Perhaps the first really popular small bus for the owner driver after the end of the First World War was the American Model T Ford, one of the most famous chassis of all time. It was even more favoured after it had an extension to its frame fitted from a kit supplied by either Eto, Eros, Olsen, or more usually Baico. This added a further 3 ft. 6 ins to the chassis by fixing on a steel extension made out of 3 inch by 2 inch channels and with overall dimensions of 9 ft 5 ins. by 2 ft. 10 ins. This was supported by a pair of 44 inch by 2¼ inch semi-elliptical springs attached to side brackets which

in turn were mounted on the main frame extension and supported on special spring saddles forming parts of two heavy castings. Baico exhibited such an extension fitted to a 20-seat coach at the 1921 Commercial Motor Show.

The Model T bus went on for a long time and as late as 1927 RT 2975 appeared with a Trice (Ipswich) 14-seat bus body. Trice were one of a host of small coachbuilders who undertook such work. Others included Swannick and Chadwick and some operators built their own bodies to their own specifications.

In the 'thirties the T finally gave way to two other Fords, the AA that could have either a 14-seat body (like UR 6940) or a 20-seat one (as with JH 107); the BB was the larger version capable of having either a 20-seat body (e.g. BKP 296) or a 26-seat one (e.g. GTW 168). Generally speaking 1935 marks the dividing line between the earlier AA and the later BB models.

**Garrett O**

The Garrett O type was a two-axle trolleybus which found favour with several systems in the mid-'twenties. At the 1925 Olympia one was displayed with a 36-seat single-deck body and was powered by one Bull 50 h.p. motor. It interested Bradford Corporation who ordered four in 1926. One may well have been the above-mentioned Show model. for No. 535 had an East Suffolk registration (RT 1345). The other three, (Nos. 532–4, KU 9101–3), were in fact, fitted with B.T.H. motors. Another municipality to try out the Garrett O that year was Ipswich, who took delivery of fifteen of these, all with Garrett's own 31-seat dual entrance/exit bodywork. Nos. 22–35 (DX 5622–30/2–7, but not in that sequence) were followed in 1927 by the first trolleybuses to be run by St. Helens Corporation (Nos. 1–4, DJ 3243–6), and these had 35-seat Ransomes central entrance bodies and Bull motors.

1927 was also the year when Bradford placed a repeat order for the O; No. 536 (UM 1755) may have been destined for Leeds but Nos. 537–9 (KW 204–6) were certainly made for Bradford. All had Roe bodywork and Bull motors. In 1927 West Hartlepool Corporation took delivery of one dozen Os with 32-seat Roe bodies, Nos. 20–31 (EF 3370–81), which were powered by 50 h.p. Bull motors.

During 1928 Mexborough & Swinton began to take into their ranks Garrett Os with that manufacturer's 32-seat central entrance bodies. Nos. 34–9 (WW 4688–93) and 40–8 (WW 7872–80) appeared that year, Nos. 49–60 (WW 8790–801) followed the next year and Nos. 61–3 (WX 4440–2) in 1930, the same year that Ipswich bought their last Garrett (No. 45, DX 9610). Thereafter the name Garrett seems to vanish from the p.s.v. scene.

### Garrett OS

At the 1927 Commercial Motor Show Garrett introduced their OS model. This was a six-wheeler with a wheelbase of 15 ft. 6 ins. and an overall length of 25 ft. 10 ins. It was powered by a single 60 h.p. Bull motor and had a 55-seat highbridge body. Doncaster took four of these in 1928 (Nos. 1–4, DT 821–4) with B.T.H. motors and 60-seat Roe bodywork. However, the OS was never as successful a proposition as the earlier and smaller O model.

### Gilford F and Successors

In May 1925 E. Horne & Company Ltd,. of Holloway Road in London, began to produce commercial vehicles under the trade name Gilford. These chassis were largely of Garford origin, for as K. C. Blacker reveals in an article in *Buses Illustrated* (February 1960): 'In fact, throughout their existence, the Gilford workshops never manufactured anything, but simply assembled ready-made parts supplied by outside firms.'

It was the Gilford F type lorry chassis that began to start the p.s.v. side of their business. This was a 2½-ton model with a wheelbase of 15 ft., which made it possible to fit a bus body carrying from 22 to 26 seated passengers. The engine chosen was an American Buda 4 cylinder side valve of 4·32 litres capacity (bore 4 in.; stroke 5¼ in.), which developed 44 b.h.p. at 1,600 r.p.m. The gearbox was part of the engine and drove a three-piece propeller shaft to an underslung worm.

In the following year (1926) a 14 ft. wheelbase version of the F was marketed as the Swift and this was capable of carrying 20 passengers.

At the same time a 6 cylinder Buda engine was installed in their new LLC range. These initials seem to stand for Lowline Coach which was sometimes referred to as the Gilford 'Safety' coach presumably because of its low chassis height from the ground. It came in two models, the smaller (later called the LL15, since it had a 15 ft. wheelbase) was powered by a 5·8 litre engine with a bore of 3⅞ in. and a stroke of 5 in., developing 57·5 b.h.p. This normally carried 26 passengers which was the case with those supplied to Perth Corporation and given Croall bodywork (Nos. 23–5, ES 9938/94/30). The larger form of the LLC became the LL166 (i.e. wheelbase of 16 ft. 6 ins.); it had a 6·3 litre engine with a bore of 4 in. and a stroke of 5⅛ in., and was capable of receiving 30-seat bodies. One of these appeared at the 1927 Olympia Show with a Strachan & Brown 20-seat coach body which incorporated a raised observation platform at the rear, a toilet and a kitchen!

In 1928 the LL15 was renamed the 15 SD (meaning Standard Drive or as we usually call it, normal control) and a forward control version, the 15OT, was added to the range. In this instance OT stood for Over Type, another rare term in British bus circles.

**Gilford 166 Series.** Pl. 111

New in 1928 were the 166SD and the 166OT. Both normal control and forward control models had a new American engine, the 6 cylinder 36 h.p. side valve Lycoming. This unit had a 5·8 litre swept volume, with a bore of $3\frac{7}{8}$ in. and a stroke of 5 in. Transmission was through a 4 speed gearbox and multiple plate clutch. The rear axle was a Kirkstall fully-floating type and four-wheel brakes were fitted. As their designation indicates these chassis had a 16 ft 6 ins. wheelbase. Approximately 730 of the 15SD/OT and 166SD/OT models were sold in the period up to and including 1930. Some of the first vehicles in the fleet of Black & White Motorways were 166SDs (Nos. 16–18, DF 5337/8 and 5559) with their 26-seat front entrance London Lorries coach bodies. These were followed by an equal number of the 166OT version (Nos. 19–21, DF 5734–6) with similar bodies. Westminster Coaching Services bought a trio of 166OTs (GK 3409–11) in 1930 which had Gilford's own 31-seat coach bodies constructed by their subsidiary Wycombe Motor Bodies Ltd. (Gilfords had moved to High Wycombe, Bucks, in 1927).

In 1933–4 the newly formed L.P.T.B. were to acquire many of the 166 series of Gilfords from small and medium size operators working in their huge area. These formed their GF class. Thus GF 1–13 came from Skylark Motor Coaches of London, W.1 and they were of the SD type which had worked express routes from Oxford Circus to Hertford Heath, Guildford and High Wycombe. GF 19–22 were of the OT variety and hailed from Regent Motor Services who operated them on the Oxford Circus–Enfield–Hertford route. GF24/5 were OTs from Buck Expresses of Watford, and thus the pattern of acquiring these coaches went on in this vein. However, by far the largest fleet of 166s entered the ranks of Hillmans of Romford. Nos. 1–12

and 87/8 were of the forward control model.

In 1929 the wheelbase was extended by 2 ins. thus introducing the 168 series. This had a slightly more powerful Lycoming engine of 6·0 litres in which the bore had been increased by $\frac{1}{16}$ in. Black & White Motorways continued to patronise Gilfords, purchasing ten of the 168SD model (Nos. 41–50) and six of the 168OT variety. (Nos. 61–6, DG 1909–14). In the latter case Wycombe bodies were fitted instead of London Lorries. Once again Hillmans took many of the 168 series, Nos. 13–49/52–82 were all 26-seat 168OTs.

In 1932 168MOT appeared using a more powerful Meadows (hence the added M) 6 cylinder engine with overhead valves which could develop 115 b.h.p. Hillmans continued purchasing Nos. 83/4, 90–3, 107–18 and 120–4 being 168MOTs.

**Gilford Hera**

1933 saw the birth of the Gilford 176S (at High Wycombe S stood for Single-decker), otherwise called the Hera. This longer wheelbase chassis (17 ft. 6 ins.) had a new 6 cylinder Vulcan Juno 7·4 litre petrol engine to power it. S.M.T. ordered some, but with Leyland units fitted, and these became known as L176S models. Hillmans only bought two, CNO 75/6 in 1935. A Tangye 6 cylinder oil engine was optional with the Hera. Later the Dorman 6 cylinder diesel unit was also offered, but by this time Gilfords were losing ground to their competitors and the writing was on the wall. Blacker* points to two cogent reasons for this decline in their fortunes: 'Gilford staff had to go out to intercept and confiscate vehicles on the road for which payment had not been made. The last reason is the loss of many good customers due to the formation of the London Transport Passenger Board.'
*Buses Illustrated* (May 1960).

The L.P.T.B. had, in fact, bought up 220 Gilfords.

## Gilford 6WOT

The name means Six-Wheeler Over Type and this model was designed to carry 40 passengers, thus competing with other contemporary models produced by Guys, Karriers and other manufacturers. It had yet another brand of American engine, the Wisconsin 6 cylinder side-valve unit. Not many of the 6WOT were ever built during its brief reign of 1928–30. Russells bought a pair for their London–Folkestone express service, which had both kitchen and toilet facilities. A 33-seat Duple-bodied 6WOT was operated by Askew & Sons on their London–Plymouth route. Even sweet and cigarette vending machines were installed in this particular vehicle.

The wheelbase of the 6WOT was 16 ft. 6 ins., and the rear axles 3 ft. 10 ins. It had drive only on the forward of the rear axles. Braking was hydraulically assisted. The chassis frame was of 'spectacle' shape as on other six-wheelers of this period.

## Gilford Front Wheel Drive

At the 1931 Olympia Gilfords displayed two revolutionary vehicles. Perhaps the reason which, above all others, makes their mention a 'must' in any history of the period, is that they were the only front wheel drive buses ever to be built in this country. Secondly, their height was phenomenally low. Using flat floors in both saloons the 56-seat Wycombe double-deck version still managed to be only 12 ft. 11 ins. By dispensing with driven rear axles the chassis could be lowered by over 1 ft. However, the internal dimensions, especially of the upper saloon (5 ft. 8½ ins.) were more appropriate for 'diddy-men'. The single-deck model had an overall height of a mere 7 ft. 10 ins. for similar reasons. Both models were powered by a Junkers

6 cylinder *two stroke* oil engine of 5·87 litres, with a bore of 77 mm and a stroke of 210 mm, all of which led to 120 b.h.p. at 2,000 r.p.m. Apparently due to difficulties over manufacturing rights, at Olympia the double-decker had dummy wooden pistons fitted (according to K. C. Blacker writing in *Buses Illustrated*, April 1960). He also describes the unorthodox emergency exit on this vehicle: 'The position of the upper-deck emergency exit . . . was in the form of a hinged door, several feet in height and mounted at the level of the platform separating the lower and upper halves of the staircase, and only 5 ft. 5 ins. from the ground when the vehicle was laden.' Gruss air springs were fitted, four at the rear and two more near the ends of the front axle.

Because it was so far ahead of its time (like the A.E.C. Q and the Leyland Gnu) both these forward drive buses were unwanted. Although the double-decker was registered as JD 1942 and appeared in the livery of Hillmans of Romford (as their No. 100) it never seems to have worked as a motorbus. Instead its fate was to be converted in September 1932, to be repainted in Wolverhampton livery and to be re-registered JW 2347. It received a 70 b.h.p. Electric Construction Company motor mounted in the same lower saloon casing as that which had housed the diesel unit. In addition to Lockheed hydraulic four-wheel brakes, automatic electric brakes were fitted and these had regenerative action at speeds over 14 m.p.h. It ran in the above fleet between 17 November and 31 December before being sold to Southend Corporation. The single-decker never even worked and when Gilfords were wound up in 1937 it was sold as scrap for £7 10s.

## Gilford Zeus

The first Zeus chassis was seen in 1932 at the Scottish Show in Glasgow and it was later fitted with a 54-seat Strachans body.

Known as the 163D it had, of course, a wheelbase of 16 ft. 3 ins. which made it capable of carrying a 56-seat body. The following year at Olympia another Zeus appeared with a 56-seat Beadle body. Although the 163D was designed to be powered by a Vulcan 'Juno' engine (this was a 6 cylinder oil unit with a bore/stroke of 110 mm/130 mm, giving a capacity of 7·4 litres), in actual fact the Show vehicle was given a Tangye 6 cylinder oil engine with a 101·6 mm bore and 127 mm stroke and so was referred to as a T163D model. One of these Zeus double-deckers went to Alexanders who ran WG 1619 for only a fortnight before returning it to Gilfords. Later it was sold to Western S.M.T. as their No. 723. At this time (1934) Western had bought a new Zeus (No. 722, CS 122). It is believed that instead of Tangye engines they were given Leyland oil units. Another Zeus seems to have gone into the fleet of Hillmans of Romford.

## G.N.R. - Gardner 5LW

Up until 1936 the Great Northern Railway in Ireland had built, at its Dundalk works, bodies for some of its fleet. For example the Leyland Tigers Nos. 263/4 (ZI 8544/5), the Dennis Aces Nos. 33–7 (ZA 3827–9 and 7154/5) and the A.E.C. Regal II No. 61 (ZA 7156) had all received G.N.R. bodies before entering service. Now for the first time in Ireland an operator was going to construct the chassis as well. All models would be fitted with the Gardner 5LW engine. The first of this breed started on routes early in 1937 and consisted of four buses with 27-seat rear entrance bodywork (Nos. 200–3, ZC 197–200). They were soon followed by Nos. 204–7 (ZC 1289–92), which this time had 32-seat rear entrance bodies. The third batch (Nos. 208–11, ZC 1576–9) were similar. The fourth quartet (Nos. 212–15, ZC 1848–51) had a mixed seating capacity, for

while 212 had 32, 215 had one less, and the middle two had as many as 35 seats. This total was adopted for the 1937 final group, Nos. 216–19 (ZC 2267–70).

In 1938 production of 35-seaters continued apace as the following list indicates. However, Nos. 247–50 originally had only 31 seats.

| Fleet No. | Registration No. |
|-----------|------------------|
| 220 | FZ 831 |
| 241 | ZC 3823 |
| 242/4/5 | ZC 4102–4 |
| 243/6—8 | ZC 4396–9 |
| 249–52 | ZC 4572–5 |
| 253–7 | ZC 4731–5 |
| 258/9 | ZC 5472/3 |

Meanwhile some of the earlier G.N.R. Gardners had been re-designed to seat 35. It was over two years before any more of this type were constructed. In 1941 the final batch of 'pre-war' (if that is not a misnomer?) G.N.R. Gardners appeared on the scene. These were Nos. 318–27 (ZD 720–9) which also had 35 seats apiece.

## Guy Runabout. Pl. 25

Before Guys commenced with their main bus manufacturing interests in 1924 they did build the J lorry chassis which was suitable for small bus bodies. Birkenhead Corporation used one (No. 38, CM 6045) fitted with Guy's own 20-seater front entrance bus body, but that was as late as 1925. However, it was in 1923 that Bournemouth put into service, between Bournemouth Pier and Boscombe Pier, three J chassis with locally built J. & A. Steane 16-seat toastrack bodies. (Nos. 1–3, EL 8127–9). Their success on route 15 resulted in them being joined by a further three Runabouts in the following summer (Nos. 4–6, EL 9424–6). Portsmouth also wanted Runabouts for their seafront route between Clarence Pier and South Parade Pier, Southsea; Nos. 11–15 (TP 115/7/9/8/6) had 15-seat toastrack bodies built by Wadhams of nearby Waterlooville.

The first small capacity chassis, purpose built for p.s.v. operation by Guys, was the OWD in 1926. This had a wheelbase initially, of 11 ft. 6 ins., and was powered by a small 4 cylinder engine with bore/stroke measurements of 88 mm/ 120 mm. By the 1927 Commercial Motor Show the wheelbase had been extended to 12 ft. 5 ins. so that the seating capacity could be raised from 16 to 20. Walsall Corporation took delivery of an 18-seater on an OWD chassis in 1926 (No. 38, DH 4782).

In 1929 the OWD was replaced by two similar models called the OND (normal control) and the ONDF (forward control). However, both vehicles were built with half-cabs. Wolverhampton Corporation chose the former model for their Nos. 75/6 (UK 5975/6) and 81/4 (UK 6581/4) and West Bromwich Corporation selected the forward control version for their Nos. 25–7 (EA 4193–5). All seven vehicles had 20-seater Guy bodywork fitted. Finally in 1932 a longer form of the OND appeared as the ONDL. When the optional 6 cylinder 3·6 litre engine was preferred then the ONDL was called the Victory. This small unit had a bore of 80 mm and a stroke of 120 mm. At the close of 1933 these were, in turn, displaced by the new Wolf and Vixen range of small bus/coach chassis.

## Guy BA Series. Pl. 26

It was in 1924 that Guy Motors of Wolverhampton introduced their first chassis designed specifically for bus use in the form of a trio known as the BA, the B and the BB. All had the same kind of dropped frame chassis and the main difference lay in their respective wheelbases of 13 ft. 4 ins., 15 ft. 3 ins. and 16 ft. 5 ins. They all had worm driven rear axles. They also shared the 4·5 litre 4 cylinder engine with a bore of 4 in.

and a stroke of 5½ in. The BA was suitable for 20-seater bodies and Burton-on-Trent Corporation invested in a couple of these vehicles in 1924 as their Nos. 1/2 (FA 1820/1) with Guy's own 20-seat front entrance bodywork. They followed up this order with a series of the B model each fitted with 25-seater Guy bodies, although Nos. 7–9 (FA 2237–9) seated only 20, and Nos. 1/2 (FA 2731/2) seated 26. Other buyers of the BB included Keighley Corporation with No. 26 (WT 5647) seating 28, No. 27 (WT 6669) seating 20 and Nos. 37–40 (WU 452/ 3/1/0) seating 26. Leicester Corporation's Nos. 15–18 (RY 4373–6), 30–3 (RY 5551–4), 40–3 (RY 7695–8) and 44–6 (RY 7851–3) had 25-seat Brush bodies. National Omnibus & Transport Company purchased five (Nos. 2306/7/11/5 and 2416), the last numbered possessing a 26-seat London Lorries coach body.

The larger BB version found favour with Walsall Corporation. Their Nos. 39–43 (DH 4900–4) and 59/60 (DH 5900–1) had 31-seat rear or 30-seat front entrance Vickers bodywork. Nearby West Bromwich Corporation tried out three with Guy 30-seater bodies (Nos. 11, EA 3200; No. 12, EA 3334; No. 14, EA 3535). Birkenhead Corporation's Nos. 52–4 (CM 6608–10) were given Guy 26-seat dual entrance/exit bodies. After an initial batch consisting of Nos. 24–30 (FA 3856–62), Burton-on-Trent had Gardner 4LW engines fitted to a further pair (Nos. 42/3, FA 5447/8). By the 1927 Olympia Show the BB's engine had been increased in size to have a bore of 4¼ in. This brought it into line with the FBB model which had appeared in 1926. This was Guy's first forward control bus chassis. Because of the revised position of the driver it was possible to seat more passengers. West Bromwich's 1929 vintage FBBs sat 36 (Nos. 16, EA 3800; 18/9, EA 3861; 20–4, EA 4071–5). Wolverhampton Corporation also bought two of the FBB model; Nos. 55/6 (UK

2755/6) were fitted with 35-seat rear entrance Dodson bodies. On the other hand A. & W. of Harrow ordered their pair of FBBs (MP 5344 and MY 8142) with only 29-seat bodies.

So far all the Guy single-deck models mentioned have been powered by 4 cylinder engines, but in 1925, Guy brought out their 6 cylinder version known as either the BK or else as the Premier Six. It had the same chassis frame as the BB. The Daimler-Knight engine had the same 5·76 litre engine that powered the huge A.D.C. 802 double-decker. This had a bore of 97 mm and a stroke of 130 mm and had originally been used for the Daimler 35 h.p. car. National Omnibus & Transport called for five of the BK, which became Nos. 2301/3/4/12/4 in their fleet. Each had a 25-seat front entrance body.

## Guy BX Series

Guy astounded many people in 1926 by placing on the market a six-wheeled normal control double-decker powered by a 4 cylinder engine. This side valve unit had a bore of $4\frac{1}{4}$ in. and a stroke of $5\frac{1}{2}$ in., giving a capacity of 5·1 litres. It was designed to seat 62 passengers, a great number for the mid-'twenties. While local Wolverhampton Corporation were trying out a BX with a Dodson body (No. 47, DA 9047), Birmingham Corporation also sampled one, their No. 208 (OP 237) which received a 56-seat Short Bros. body.

By the 1927 Olympia Show Guy had already improved on the BX and offered it there in a choice of three wheelbase lengths, i.e. 16 ft. 7 ins. (for 60-seat double-deckers), 18 ft. 6 ins. (suitable for 70-seat double-deckers) and 19 ft. $1\frac{1}{2}$ ins. (for either a 74-seat double-decker or a 39-seat single-decker). There were other variations offered. The normal control model was re-engined with a Daimler-Knight 6 cylinder unit of 5·76 litres developing 100 b.h.p. at 2,300 r.p.m.

and called the BKX; a forward control version of this became the FBKX. A 4 cylinder forward control model also appeared in the catalogues and was referred to as the FBX. Foremost among those buying the FBKX version double-decker were the newly established Public Omnibus Company of London (62 seats), Manchester Corporation (66 seats), Liverpool, Blackpool (40 seats), Rotherham (40 seats) and Salford (38 seats).

From 1928 a new 6 cylinder side valve engine was introduced into all the larger Guy models, which were then made available in the following forms:—

| Model | Control | Wheels | Wheelbase | Seats |
|-------|---------|--------|-----------|-------|
| C | Normal | 4 | 16 ft. 5 ins. | 28 |
| FC | Forward | 4 | 16 ft 5 ins. | 32 |
| CX | Normal | 6 | 16 ft. 7 ins | 32 |
| CX | Normal | 6 | 18 ft. 6 ins. | 66 |
| CX | Normal | 6 | 19 ft. $1\frac{1}{2}$ ins. | 39 |
| CX | Normal | 6 | 19 ft. $1\frac{1}{2}$ ins. | 72 |
| FCX | Forward | 6 | same variations as for CX | |

Of the ten possible permutations, some did not last very long. The first to go by 1929 were the CX choices, since forward control began to supersede normal control, save for touring coaches. The FCX single-deck versions also disappeared during 1929. From 1931 the single-deck FC buses/coaches became known as Conquests and their double-deck counterparts took on the title Invincible.

When we turn to operators of this sequence we find the C in the fleet of Birmingham Corporation in 1929, when Nos. 51–60 (OF 3960–9) arrived with their Guy 25-seat front entrance bodywork. These were followed by a similar batch (Nos. 61–80, OF 6071–90) in 1930. Burton-on-Trent was another municipality to take in the C. Nos. 34–41 (FA 3887–94) had 26-seat Guy bodies.

The CX found a home at Leicester where the civic fathers deemed it prudent to invest in several of these, all fitted with 56-seat Brush bodies. No. 19 (RY 4377) arrived in 1927, Nos. 20–9 (RY 5541–50) in 1928 and Nos. 47–52 (RY 7854–9) in 1929 Wolverhampton Corporation bought a series of CXs during 1928 (namely Nos. 51/7–64/67–72).

The FCX went to Wolverhampton too in the shape of No. 65 (UK 5365) with a 59-seat Brush body. National bought one with a Dodson 64-seat open stairs body (No. 2387, TM 1401).

The FC turned up in the ranks of Silcox of Pembroke Dock with a Guy 32-seat rear entrance body (No. 4, DE 9301), as well as at West Bromwich, where No. 17 (EA 3808) had a 35-seat front entrance Guy body.

In 1933 the Arab range of larger p.s.vs replaced the Conquest and the Invincible.

**Guy BT Series Trolleybuses.** Pl. 28, 117, 118

It was in 1926 that Guy Motors started to manufacture trolleybuses. Their initial model was the world's first trolleybus to be fitted with pneumatic tyres. It also incorporated regenerative control, whereby as the driver removed his foot from the power pedal and applied the brake, so the motor became a generator feeding the current back into the wires and thus acting as an additional braking force. The BT32 was a two-axle single-deck model designed to seat 32 passengers. Its wheelbase was 17 ft. $3\frac{1}{2}$ ins. and the overall body length could be up to 27 ft. 6 ins. This was not so popular as other versions. One demonstrator with a Guy front entrance body (UK 9601) ended up as No. 316 in the fleet of Notts & Derby Traction. Wolverhampton Corporation, who patronised the locally built trolleybuses, purchased four BT32s in 1934 and had Nos. 210–13 (JW 4310–13) fitted with rear entrance Park Royal bodywork.

The second model was the BT48 which was the double-deck version of the BT32 but, in spite of its number designa-

tion, it could seat up to 54 passengers. Its wheelbase was 16 ft. $3\frac{1}{2}$ ins. and its overall body length was 26 ft. There did not seem to be much demand for this model either except from Wolverhampton Corporation who bought twenty-three.

By far the most successful Guy trolleybus was the BTX. This had three axles. The BTX60 was 26 ft. long and the BTX66 a foot longer. The suffix figures did denote maximum seating capacity in these two instances. In 1935 the BTX66 was lengthened to 30 ft. which meant that it could carry 70 passengers seated. Nevertheless most BTXs seem to have carried less than these figures. South Lancs equipped their trolleybus fleet with the BTX during the period 1930–3. All forty-six vehicles had Roe lowbridge bodywork seating from 56–58 passengers. Nos. 1–30 were powered by Metro-Vick 90 h.p. motors and Nos. 31–46 had G.E.C. 80 h.p. units. Wolverhampton Corporation's BTX No. 33 (UK 633) with its 61-seat Dodson body with an open staircase was, in fact, Guy's first-born trolleybus. It was followed, over the next nine years, by a whole procession of BTXs, Nos. 34–88, 99, 200–3, 218–21 and 227–30. These had a motley collection of bodies by Dodson, Guy, Beadle, M.C.W. and Brush, seating between 58–61 passengers.

Derby Corporation bought BTX60s between 1932–4. Nos. 79–84 (RC 401–6) and 149–58 (RC 4349–58) had Brush bodywork. Nos. 85–92 (RC 544–51) and 93–8 (RC 793–8) Dodson bodywork and Nos. 102–13 (RC 1102–13) had bodies constructed by Weymanns. All seated 56 passengers. Hastings Tramways had the distinction of having the only open top BTXs built which were Nos. 1–8 (DY 4953/4/65–70) with their 57-seat Dodson bodies. Of these No. 3 still exists, albeit 'Happy Harold' now moves by means of a Rootes TS3 diesel engine!

Hastings Tramways took advantage of

the alternative form of the BTX60 which made it suitable for single-deck bodywork. Indeed, before 1945 most of the Hastings fleet consisted of BTX60s with Ransomes, Sims & Jefferies 32-seat central entrance bodies. These came in three instalments, Nos. 9–38 (DY 5111–40) in 1928; 39–48 (DY 5452–61) in 1929; and 49–58 (DY 5576–85) in 1930.

Some of the first Guy trolleybuses had Rees-Stevens electrical equipment but, after these initial vehicles, the majority of Guy trolleybuses had their equipment made by another Wolverhampton firm, Electrical Construction Company. The motor in Guy trolleybuses was mounted on the front axle although it was driving only the rear axle, thus making the propeller shaft extra long.

## Guy Arab. Pl. 110–116

In 1933 Guy introduced three new chassis all bearing the name of Arab. Each was suffixed by the number of seats expected for bodies mounted on these models. The FD32 had a wheelbase of 16 ft. 7½ ins. and an overall body length of 26 ft., measurements that were duplicated in the FD48, the double-deck version. The third member was the FD35 with its wheelbase of 17 ft. 7½ ins. and an overall body measurement of 27 ft. 6 ins. All three had 4 speed gearboxes mounted half-way along the offside of the chassis in place of the more orthodox nearside position. The FD32 and FD35 were offered with a choice of being driven by either the Gardner 4LW or the 5LW diesel engine and the latter was suggested for the FD48 along with the Gardner 6LW. Normally, customers for the FD32 and FD35 chose the 5LW and those for the FD48 the 6LW unit. However, Wolverhampton Corporation chose the 5LW for both Nos. 194/5 (JW 5794/5) of the FD32 variety and for No. 312 (JW 8112), an FD48 (seating incidentally 52). Birmingham Corporation sampled one FD48 (with a M.C.W. 50-seat body) as their No. 208 (OC 8208) in 1934 but ordered no more. Southampton Corporation also tried out some FD48s before deciding to buy a quantity of Titans. Burton-on-Trent Corporation continued their life-long patronage of Guy with purchases of FD32s and FD35s in 1936, followed by more FD32s in 1940–1.

From 1935 the Cotal electro-magnetically-controlled epicyclic gearbox was available as an option. A six-wheeler version of the Arab, designated the FDX60, was a non-starter as far as the home market was concerned, as by the mid-'thirties six-wheelers were 'out'.

In 1942 the Ministry of Supply announced that Guy had been given permission to recommence production of the Arab. During the ensuing twelve months work must have gone on almost non-stop at their works, for five hundred of the new Mark I were to come off the assembly lines. Compared with the pre-war Arab the chassis weight had gone up by 18½ per cent. due to the substitution of steel parts for aluminium ones. At the same time the transmission was shifted to the nearside and the wheelbase was reduced by 4½ ins. to 16 ft. 3 ins. All but forty of the Arab Is were originally given Gardner 5LW units, the remainder receiving the 8·4 litre 6LW instead, needed for the heavier war-time weight, plus full loads. Some operators were sampling Guys for the first time. Such were the cases of Southdown with their Nos. 400/1 (GCD 974/5), Devon General with No. 240 (HTA 740) and Gosport & Fareham with No. 55 (EHO 228). Darlington Triumph had never operated double-deck vehicles before but, with so many servicemen to shift, they took four Arab Is (Nos. DO 60–3, GHN 430–3). L.P.T.B. started a new G class for them which quickly reached G71 with Arab Is alone. Independents like Ledgards (JUA 762) and Bartons (Nos. 427–30) were treated the same as large municipalities such as Glasgow (Nos. 51–8) and Edinburgh (Nos. G4–6).

A wide variety of coachbuilding firms were asked to build the standardised 56-seat bodies with wooden slatted seats, lack of proper destination blind boxes, grey painted 'livery' and other signs of the totality of modern war. London Transport found their Mark Is arriving with bodies built by Park Royal, Northern Counties, Weymanns and Duple, and Glasgow's came from the benches of Brush, Northern Counties and Pickering. Others to be called upon in this massive effort were Massey, Strachan and Roe.

In 1943 it was decided that, to facilitate the installation of a 6 cylinder engine, the chassis should be lengthened by 5 ins. thus making the total overall length 26 ft. 5 ins., which broke the existing law. So an emergency regulation was issued, temporarily extending the total permitted body length for a two-axle double-decker, to 26 ft. 9 ins., as from 1 June 1942. This was repealed as from 1 May 1947. In that time over 2,000 of the Mark II Arab came off the production line and few operators escaped their share of these buses. To Southdown's two Mark Is were added 98 Mark IIs and London Transport's original 71 swelled to 435. Even Midland Red, who normally built their own vehicles, had to accept some Arab IIs. After their initial batch of Mark Is, (Nos. 2452–7, GHA 886–91), there followed several batches of Mark IIs throughout 1943 (Nos. 2497–508), GHA 921–32), 1944 (Nos. 2550–78, HHA 2–30) and 1945 (Nos. 2580–90, HHA 57–85).

## Guy Wolf

At the close of 1933 two new, small normal control buses were introduced by Guy. These both bore the name of Wolf. The CF14 had a wheelbase of 10 ft. 6 ins. and could carry 14 passengers. The

CF20 had a wheelbase of 12 ft. 6 ins. and could likewise accommodate 20 passengers. They were built in fairly small numbers until 1940, being powered by a 4 cylinder petrol engine of 3·31 litres (bore 90 mm; stroke 130 mm). Llandudno U.D.C. purchased two of the CF20 model, one of which (JC 5313), with its Waveney body, was still in service until the mid-'sixties and has since been preserved. Aberdeen Corporation purchased a pair of Wolves in 1934 as their Nos. 1/2 (RG 4541/2).

The larger form of this 4 cylinder petrol engined bus was called the Vixen. The Vixen 24 had a wheelbase of 12 ft 6 ins. but the Vixen 26 had this extended to 14 ft. 9 ins.

## Karrier WL6 Series. Pl. 30

At the 1925 Olympia Show Karriers introduced their six-wheeler range. The 6 cylinder engine had a bore of $3\frac{5}{16}$ in. and a stroke of $5\frac{1}{2}$ in., developing 50 b.h.p. at 1,200 r.p.m. Air pressure brakes were fitted to this normal control chassis which had the so-called 'spectacle' side-members (see p. 148 on E6 trolleybus). The wheelbase was 17 ft. thus allowing for a 28-seat single-deck body or a 54-seat double-deck body to be fitted. During 1926 this chassis appeared in an improved form, known as the WL6, of which subsequently 160 were built before 1930. For one thing the wheelbase was extended to 17 ft. 6 ins. and a Dorman 6·597 litre 6JUL engine was fitted with bore/stroke measurements of 110 mm/140 mm. It was possible to fit a 40-seat single-deck bus body on the WL6. In 1928 the catalogues suggest that the seating capacity of the WL6 was now only 37 and a new model, (WL6/1), with a 19 ft. wheelbase, was said to be the new 40-seater version. Blackpool bought one of these as their No. 51 (FR 8440) carrying a Northern Counties body. Bournemouth took five of this type (Nos.

31–5) and Edinburgh seven (Nos. 172 and 526–31).

The double-deck form of the WL6/1 was the WL6/2. Doncaster Corporation tried a pair of these large buses in 1928 with the inevitable Roe bodies, (seating 60), as their Nos. 58/9 (DT 1321/2) and Portsmouth Corporation invested in three lots of WL6/2s, Nos. 40–2 (TP 4703–5) and 43–7 (TP 4832–6) with Brush bodywork in 1927; Nos. 48–53 (TP 6872–7) with English Electric bodies in 1928. Manchester had Ransomes, Sims & Jefferies 66-seat bodies put on their WL6/2s in 1927. Sixty-six seats were also provided by Short Bros. in the body they constructed for Birmingham Corporation's solitary WL6/2 (No. 209, OP 238).

The WL6/2 was superseded by the DD6 in 1928. As well as keeping the 17 ft. 6 ins. wheelbase model the DD6 also included a 19 ft. wheelbase version suitable for bodies containing as many as 72 seats and known as the DD6/1. In 1929 the DD6 was titled the Consort. However, the days of six-wheelers were strictly numbered as we enter the 'thirties. Huddersfield Corporation, who ran the routes in Karrier's home town, bought a few with a greatly reduced wheelbase of 15 ft. 6 ins. in 1930 and bearing 56-seat Park Royal bodies.

The WL6/1 became known as the Clipper as from 1929. Blue Bird Services of South Wales bought UH 4105, a dual entrance/exit Clipper, in 1931.

## Karrier CL6 Series.

The smaller brother of the WL6 was the CL6 with a wheelbase of 15 ft. 6 ins. This was powered by what was, presumably, a Karrier 6 cylinder unit with a bore of $3\frac{3}{8}$ in. and a stroke of $4\frac{1}{2}$ in. which developed 47 b.h.p. at 1,200 r.p.m. The CL6 could be supplied as either a normal or a forward control chassis. It was designed to seat 32 passengers.

Production only lasted from 1927 until some time in 1928, during which interval only thirty chassis were assembled. Two of these went to Portsmouth Corporation and were given Ransomes, Sims & Jefferies bodies with a front entrance. They were forward control buses numbered 38/9 (TP 4812/3) in that fleet. Ashton-under-Lyne Corporation purchased three normal control CL6s and had smart 26-seat Short Bros. bodywork fitted. One of these was No. 5 (TE 3556). Stephen Whittaker & Sons, trading under the legend Violet Motors, bought a normal control CL6 and had a coach body fitted by London Lorries in 1928.

## Karrier E6

E for Electric and 6 for six wheels explains the designation of Karrier's first venture into the world of the trolleybus. Powered by Clough–B.T.H. motors the first E6s went to Doncaster Corporation in 1928 as their Nos. 5–10 (DT 2002/3, 2165–8, 2633) fitted with Roe 60-seat bodies with rear entrances. Through the years Doncaster took a further fifty-seven E6 trolleybuses with Roe 60-seat bodies. The vehicles concerned were Nos. 11–16 (DT 1745–50) in 1929; 17–23 (DT 1099, 1118, 1143, 1146, 1193 and 1206) in 1930; 24–30 (DT 3153–9) in 1931; 32 (DT 4718) in 1934; 33–6 (DT 5772–5) in 1935; 37–42 (DT 6539–44) in 1936; 43–8 (ADT 181–6) in 1937; 49–68 (BDT 114–29/31–4) in 1939. From No. 33 onwards they received Metro-Vick motors instead of B.T.H.

The first E6s were based on the motorbus chassis WL6/2 with a shortened wheelbase of 16 ft. 10⅝ ins., which meant that a body on such a chassis could seat about 64. Meanwhile, in 1930, another corporation was taking an interest in this model, namely Nottingham, who bought No. 25 (TV 4463) fitted with a Clough motor and a Park Royal body, seating 60 passengers. An order for a similar dozen vehicles quickly followed. Other

E6s went to Nottingham in 1934 (twenty-five with 64-seat Brush bodies and ten with 64-seat M.C.W. bodies). On the other hand, in 1932, Derby tried out No. 99 (RC 799) with B.T.H. motors and a Dodson 56-seat body but never ordered any more Karriers in peacetime. 1933 was the year that Huddersfield found out the worth of the E6 when they purchased a trio (Nos. 1–3, VH 5723–5) with Park Royal 60-seat bodies. From that date they decided that the E6 answered their needs and they purchased these chassis with a variety of bodywork all seating 64 between 1934 and 1939, an aggregate for this operator of 125 such vehicles.

Although Nottingham had taken delivery of one Karrier six-wheeler in 1932 called a 6A model, the true 6A only saw the light of day in 1935 when Newcastle-upon-Tyne Corporation asked for ten of this version with a wheelbase extended to 17 ft. 9 ins., so that a 70-seat, 30 ft. long body could be carried. However, in many ways, the E6 and the E6A were dissimilar. For instance, the E6A frame was of orthodox shape while the E6 was unusual as this description by Alan Townsin in *Buses Illustrated* for January 1961 shows: 'The most distinctive feature being the "spectacle" frame side-members. These were shaped to include openings through which each rear axle projected, suspension being by two pairs of springs fitted above and below the axles on each side and pivoted on central trunnion brackets midway between the axles. An advantage of this arrangement was that less intrustion on to the body was necessary as compared to a side-member arched over both axles. On the other hand it was not possible to release the complete bogie from the frame for overhaul as can be done with the more orthodox arrangement.' The motor was mounted amidships and the drive was through worm-driven axles. Westinghouse or Peters air pressure brakes were

also a fitment of the E6 model. In the E6A the bogie was manufactured by Kirkstalls.

Newcastle was the main customer for the E6A. All their trolleys of this make had M.C.W. 60-seat bodies except for Nos. 113–18 with Roe bodywork. The lower seating capacity was due to the presence of dual entrance/exits on these vehicles. The first batch was Nos. 20–9 (BVK 810–19) in 1935, followed by other batches in 1936 (Nos. 40–3, CVK 52/DTN 141–3); 1937 (Nos. 47–56, ETN 47–56); 1938 (Nos. 85–98, FVK 85–98) and 1939–40 (Nos. 113–24, HVK 113–24). Belfast Corporation tried out two E6As with Harkness rear entrance bodies in 1937.

Altogether, 253 E6 and 53 E6A trolleybuses were manufactured between 1928 and 1940, when production ceased. Since Sunbeam had acquired Karriers by that date no more separate Karrier models were built although both the W and the post-war Sunbeam models sometimes bore Karrier plates.

### Karrier E4

The first three four-wheeled Karrier trolleybuses were sent to York in 1930. Nos. 30–2 (VY 2991–3), with their Clough motors and Roe 32-seat single-deck rear entrance bus bodies, were to restart this small system that had closed the previous year after running since 1921. Such a resumption of this form of public transport after an abandonment, at the moment, remains unique in the annals of British history. This initial batch seem to have been based on the Karrier Chaser single-deck motorbus chassis and remained the only E4 single-deckers to be built. In 1936 they went to Chesterfield Corporation as their Nos. 18–20. Two other early E4 trolleybuses went to Portsmouth; as Nos. 9/11 (RV 4657/61) they took part inthe mass trials in Pompey which eventually ended in favour of the A.E.C. 661T. Whereas

No. 9 had an English Electric body and motor No. 11 had one constructed by M.C.W. and had a B.T.H. motor. Both sat 50 passengers.

In 1936 the E4 appeared in a new form. Its wheelbase was defined as 15 ft. 6 ins., and it was made specifically for double-deck work. Only two operators, in fact, were interested in the revised E4. South Shields Corporation bought two batches, both with Weyman 56-seat bodies. The first order called for thirty-two vehicles, numbered 200–31 (CU 3589–96/3851–73), and the repeat order was for just two more. (Nos. 232/3, CU 3874/5). Bradford also purchased the E4. In 1938–9 it took into stock Nos. 677–91 (CAK 677–91), again with 56-seat Weymann bodywork. These trolleybuses were powered by English Electric motors. Finally came No. 692 (DKU 692) in 1940 with similar personal details.

The E4S version remained merely in the catalogues until 1942, when Darlington Corporation placed an order for a pair to be given East Lancs 32-seat central entrance bodies. They were numbered 1 (GHN 321) and 11 (GHN 322) and had English Electric 80 h.p. motors. The E4S had a lengthened wheelbase of 16 ft. 10 ins.

A total of fifty-seven four-wheel Karrier buses were built making it quite a rarity in a world that once numbered several thousand trolleybuses.

## Lancia Pentaiota. Pl. 31

From Italy, in the 'twenties, came a challenge from the firm of Lancia. As early as the 1921 Olympia Lancia were displaying a 25-seat charabanc. By 1925 they were selling their Z type which was suitable for 21-seat bodywork. Enterprise of Clacton, bought one of these (YH 7108) and had an Alldays bus body fitted. Whereas the Z sold for £725, a similar model, the Tetraiota, realised £800. Enterprise also bought one of the latter model in 1926 (TW 1544).

At the 1925 Commercial Motor Show Lancia exhibited their Pentaiota. This had a wheelbase of 15 ft. 6 ins. and an overall length of a fraction under 23 ft. It was 6 ft. 3 ins. wide. The Pentaiota was powered by a Lancia 30 h.p. engine with bore/stroke of 110 mm/130 mm, and developed 70 b.h.p. at 2,200 r.p.m. Transmission was through a dry clutch plate and a 4 speed gearbox. It was stated to be suitable for 28-seat bodies although, at the following Olympia, it was declared upseated to 30. Enterprise bought one as a 26-seater bus (VW 3421) and another as a 20-seater coach (VW 5015) in 1928. Three years earlier National Omnibus had also taken a 20-seater coach version of the Pentaiota as their No. 2234 (PU 7841).

## Leyland Titan. Pl. 119–130

It was at the 1927 Commercial Motor Show that Leyland introduced their new Titan TD1 double-decker. For the first time three features that were winning approval among operators were combined into one vehicle, namely, a 6 cylinder engine, low frame height and vacuum brakes. At this date the double-decked motor bus was quite a rarity outside London and Birmingham and doubtless Leyland had an eye to tramway conversion which was already in the air as far as several towns were concerned. It is interesting to note that whereas Birmingham only bought one TD1 (No. 99, OF 3959), Glasgow purchased no less than 273 of this model (Nos. 51–248/275–349), with either Leyland or Cowieson bodywork. Among other municipalities to sample the first Titan were Birkenhead (Nos. 79–125/132–52/159–63); Dundee (Nos. 35–46, TS 9117–28); Exeter (Nos. 31–40, FJ 7829–38); Keighley (Nos. 53–7, WW 5510/7422/7861-3) and Portsmouth (Nos. 4–10 and 85–94). In the ranks of company operators, Devon General bought a quartet (Nos. 38–41), and Southdown took them in large numbers starting off with Brush open top bodied ones (Nos. 801–23, UF 4801–23), and then progressing, via lowbridge bodied Leyland vehicles (Nos. 824–65, UF 5424–9/5530–41/5642–65), to highbridge versions by both Leyland (Nos. 866–77, UF 6466–77) and Short (Nos. 878–944, UF 7078–81/7382–7432/8873–84). Some of the earliest TD1s had Leyland bodies which, although possessing permanent roofs, still retained open staircases (e.g. the Keighley vehicles). Seating capacities varied from 48 to 51.

The T type engine of the TD1 had a capacity of 6·8 litres with a bore of 4 in. and a stroke of $5\frac{1}{2}$ in. The drive was through a 4 speed sliding mesh gearbox to an underslung worm driven rear axle. The wheelbase was 16 ft. 6 ins. and the overall length 25 ft.

1932 saw the emergence of the TD2 version with its improved 7·6 litre engine with a bore of $4\frac{1}{4}$ in. and a stroke of $5\frac{1}{2}$ in. Other changes included three servo- in place of single servo-brakes and fully floating rear axles as a substitute for the previous semi-floating ones. Under the 1930 Road Traffic Act four-wheeled double-deckers could be 26 ft. long, and this meant that Southdown's next two batches of Titans (Nos. 945–59, UF 8845–54/9755–9) could seat 52 passengers instead of 50. Among operators taking their first Titans in the Mark 2 form were Great Southern Railway of Ireland (RP 7–14, PI 6397–404) and Wilts & Dorset (Nos. 109–14, WV 2379–84), the latter seating only 48 in their Leyland lowbridge bodies, while the former packed in 51 seats in their own company built lowbridge bodywork. A few TD2s were fitted with oil engines.

The following year (1933) saw the TD3 on the market. This had the length from the front of the vehicle to the front bulkhead reduced from 4 ft. $11\frac{1}{2}$ ins. to 4 ft. 5 ins. and at the same time the more modern looking radiator with its parallel sides was fitted. The TD3 could therefore seat more and some operators, such as Birkenhead (Nos. 189–97, BG 2654–62), took advantage of this when they had 54-seat Northern Counties and Massey bodywork fitted to the chassis; Sheffield Corporation had 53-seat Craven bodies fitted to their Nos. 241–50 (AWB 941–50). Among newcomers into the Titan field Maidstone & District had 48-seat *central* entrance *Harrington* bodies placed on their Nos. 338–45 (BKK 302–9). One special form of the third Titan, designated the TD3c, introduced the torque converter.

Writing in *Buses Illustrated* No. 21 (January–March 1955), Alan Townsin describes this thus: 'This was based on Lysholm-Smith patents, and provided a fully-automatic transmission, apart from a manually engaged direct drive for what would normally be regarded as "top gear" conditions. The latter was controlled by a lever (replacing the normal gear lever) which had four positions, direct, converter, neutral and reverse. No clutch pedal was fitted. The "converter" position was normally employed for all conditions from the vehicle being at rest (in which case the converter acted in a similar way to a fluid flywheel) to travelling at about 20 m.p.h. at which speed the direct drive was engaged. When starting from rest the engine speed would rapidly rise to about 1,200 r.p.m. and then remain almost constant as the vehicle accelerated with the converter acting as an infinitely variable ratio drive until the speed for engaging direct drive was reached. Similarly, when climbing a hill the engine speed remained steady as the speed dropped due to the increasing gradient, and these characteristics gave a false impression of sluggish and rather fussy performance which was probably heightened by the free wheel incorporated in the converter drive. However, there was an appreciable amount of actual slip, and the energy thus lost reappeared as heat, necessitating large coolers on the side of the chassis.' Southdown were anxious to try out four of these 'gearless' buses on some of the flat routes at Worthing. Nos. 960–3 (AUF 660–3) were eventually given ordinary gearboxes (1946) and oil engines (1940) when they were modernised. Birkenhead and Sheffield also took delivery of the TD3c.

In 1935 the 3 servo-braking system was altered on the Titan to a vacuum-hydraulic one, and so was born the TD4 and the TD4c. The former found favour in the ranks of London Transport as their STD class (DLU 311–410), and also with Dublin United Tramways, who bought fifty (R 1–50, ZC 714–50/3751–63). East Kent took into their fleet two batches of diesel engined TD4 buses with 53-seat lowbridge bodywork (JG 7010–29 with Brush bodies and JG 8201–50 with Park Royal bodies). Bolton Corporation (Nos. 25–44, WH 7801–20), Glasgow (Nos. 375–434, YS 2021–80), Birmingham (Nos. 964–8, COX 964–8) and Portsmouth (Nos. 126/30, RV 6369/73) were some of the municipal operators who bought TD4c buses. Seating capacity on the TD4 varied from Maidstone & District's mere 48 up to Devon General's 56 on their Beadle bodied Nos. 230–3 (CTA 111–14). P.M.T. had some TD4s with 56-seat lowbridge bodies built by Brush (Nos. 252–66, CVT 1–10/DVT 901–5), which was high for this kind of body in 1936.

The 1937 Commercial Motor Show celebrated a decade of the Titan with the next version, the TD5 and TD5c. The wheelbase had been reduced to 16 ft 3 ins. (as it had already been in the London Transport STD class) and other minor improvements to the chassis carried out. Most of these models were equipped with an oil engine of 6·8 litres with a 4 in. bore and a 5½ in. stroke, but Bournemouth Corporation's Nos. 17–32 (FEL 200–15) of 1939 vintage with their

dual entrance/exit 48-seat Weymann bodies were powered by a 7·9 litre engine with an increased bore of 4 $\frac{6}{16}$ in.

The only TD6 and TD6c ever built went to Birmingham as their Nos. 1270–1319 (FOF 270–319) and 211–95 (EOG 211–95) respectively. They were TD5 models modified to suit that operator's requirements and were delivered in 1938–9.

Fully flexible engine mountings were the chief improvement of the TD7, which appeared just after the outbreak of the Second World War. Bolton took the first in the form of some TD7c vehicles, and both D.U.T. and G.S.R. in Eire found places for the TD7 in their ranks. The Yorkshire independent Samuel Ledgard took a trio with 56-seat Leyland bodies (JNW 288–90). However, most of the TD7 chassis were 'frozen' by the Government and when they were released during 1942 nearly 200 chassis were sent to have utility bodies and then sold to a variety of operators, some of whom had never patronised Leylands before. Thus Aldershot & District received a pair with East Lancs bodies (ECG 943/4) and Midland Red nine as their Nos. 2432–40 (GHA 786–94). Some even landed with small independents such as Hants & Sussex (ECG 616) and King Alfred of Winchester (ECG 639).

## Leyland Titanic. Pl. 34

A six-wheeled version of the Titan appeared concurrently with the TD1 and was known as the TT1. This was obviously ahead of its time, for only five were ever constructed. One of these was a Leyland demonstrator and it had a dual entrance/exit body, very similar in style to the Leyland bodies fitted to TD1s. Three other TT1s went to City Coaches as their Nos. TS1–3. They passed into the hands of the L.P.T.B. in 1933, who renumbered them as their TC class. These had open staircases and a rear entrance only. The front design was very similar to the A.E.C. Renowns of the LT class.

It was in 1934 that the TT2, being really a six-wheel version of the TD2, began to be manufactured. Again City Coaches took a trio, AGH 149–51. These had 37-seat, front entrance coach bodies built by Harringtons. Doncaster Corporation took a 'gearless' TT2c as their No. 65 (DT 5276) and had a Roe 60-seat body fitted. Doncaster subsequently took batches of TT5c buses with similar bodies in 1936 (Nos. 71–3, DT 7811–13) and 1938 (Nos. 74–9, DT 9641—3/756–8). The TT3 had a wheelbase of 17 ft. 1½ ins. and the TT4 a longer one of 18 ft. 10½ ins. They were both six-wheel versions of the Titan TD4. Likewise, the TD5 to the TT5 and the TT6, which superseded the TT3 and TT4 respectively according to wheelbase measurements.

## Leyland Lion. Pl. 133–139

It was as early as 1925 that the Lion first appeared on the transport scene. Built as basically a 32-seater single-deck bus, the PLSC1 had a 5·1 litre petrol engine with a bore of 4¼ in. and a stroke of 5½ in. Transmission was by means of a plate clutch and 4 speed sliding mesh gearbox. There was a double-reduction rear axle, made up of helical gears and a spiral bevel unit. Edinburgh Corporation was one of the first to buy this model, taking into its fleet in 1926 eight PLSC1s (Nos. 505–11) with Leyland 29-seat dual entrance/exit bodywork. Indeed, this rather modern sounding arrangement was copied by Dundee Corporation during 1927–8 with their Nos. 1–20. Glasgow took only four of this version of the Lion and these had 31-seat rear entrance bodies (Nos. 17–20). Perhaps some of the most famous and certainly longest lived PLSC1s went to J.M.T. on Jersey, whose Nos. 20/1 (J 5001/2) with 32-seat rear entrance bodies were shipped out in 1929, followed by some of the last PLSC1s produced in 1932 in the form of

Nos. 32–4 (J 1316/1297/4546). In these instances either 30-seat rear entrance bodies were fitted or else a 29-seat dual entrance/exit one.

Late in 1926 a slightly larger version of the Lion with an optimum capacity of 35 passengers seated was introduced as the PLSC3, although Wilts & Dorest squeezed a 36th seat into their Nos. 52–9/63–5 in 1927–9. In contrast the dual entrance/exit body could cope with 32, as was found by Edinburgh (Nos. 512–25) and Exeter Corporation (Nos. 1/2, FJ 6150/1). By now other body building firms were supplementing the output from the Leyland works. Devon General chose Hall Lewis for their Nos. 110–7/24–7, as did Edinburgh along with Croall and Cowieson, since quick delivery was regarded as important.

1929 saw the beginning of the replacement of the PLSC models by a new improved Lion, the LT1 with its *four* cylinder T type of petrol engine and wheelbase of 16 ft. 7¼ ins. Gradually, the differences between the Lion range and the larger Titan and Tiger series became less and less. Thus, in 1930, the LT2 was really the TS3 Tiger with the LT1 engine. The wheelbase of this model was 16 ft. 6 ins. In 1931 the LT3 appeared with this dimension increased to 17 ft. 6 ins. Some of the operators who had patronised the PLSC series continued with the LT models. Devon General, for example, had 31- or 32-seat dual entrance/exit LT1s (Nos. 128–30/46–59) and similar bodied LT2s (Nos. 170–7) before turning to 31-seat, front entrance, Park Royal bodied LT2s (Nos. 1–24). Wilts & Dorset bought Leyland bodied LT1s (Nos. 67–73/6–8) and LT2s (Nos. 91/2), before ordering some with Harrington coach bodies (Nos. 81–4). Dundee bought eight LT1s in 1930 (Nos. 21–8, TS 8413–20), and J.M.T. three LT2s a year later (Nos. 35/7/8). Across the Irish Sea the Londonderry Lough Swilly Railway took four LT2s with Leyland bodies (Nos. 1/2/5/6), and Great Northern Railway a medley with bodies by McKeown & Clughon (Nos. 112/8, AZ 5077/9), Service M.W. (Nos. 110/9/1/09, AZ 5078/80–2) and Mansons 148–51, AZ 7641–4). Improved Lions, the LT4s, went to D.U.T. as their Nos. 580–9 with operator built 36-seat rear entrance bodies in 1935; earlier Great Southern Railway had taken into stock a score of 31-seater LT4s (Nos. 712–31, ZI 8739–58).

In 1932 the LT5 made its debut. This had fully floating rear axles and three servo-brakes, thus marking the same change as in the Titan range from the TD1 to the TD2. The overall length was now standardised at 27 ft. 6 ins. Seating capacities varied from the 31 in the Weymann bodies belonging to Devon General, Nos. 32–70, up to the 36 of the D.U.T. LT5As of 1934–6. The LT5A was a variant in which the bonnet length was reduced from 4 ft 11½ ins. down to 3 ft. 11¼ ins., and at the same time, the wheelbase was lengthened by a single inch to 17 ft. 7 ins. At the same time a 5·7 litre oil engine was offered as an alternative to the petrol 4 cylinder unit of the LT series. The LT6 seems to have been another 'overseas' model for Ireland, G.S.R. buying two dozen of them and fitting their own 32-seat rear entrance bus bodies during 1934–5.

In 1935, as with the Titan and the Tiger, the Lion also was given vacuum-hydraulic brakes and consequently re-designated as the LT7. As well as serving the old faithful customers the LT7 entered the fleets of some of the larger independents such as Bartons (Nos. 196/212/4/253–67) with Duple bodies seating up to 39. Eastern Coachwork 35-seat bus bodies were given to Birch Bros., Nos. K44–7 (BLO 977/8 and CLA 102/3) in 1935. There were only minor changes in the chassis design that converted the LT7 into the LT8 in 1937. Similarly, a small increase in the wheelbase measure-

ment, to 17 ft. 8½ ins., introduced the LT9, most of which appear to have been bought by G.S.R. during the period 1938–40 (as their Nos. NP 35–79, together with ONP 12 and fourteen that bore no fleet numbers!). With the delivery of these the production of tne Lion ceased and it was not resumed in a post-war series as was the case with both the Titan and the Tiger.

## Leyland Lioness

Whereas the Lion was a forward control vehicle, its companion, the Lioness, was of the older, normal control design. Originally, in 1925, it was advertised as a 26-seater, the PLC1, powered by a smaller engine than the Lion, a 3·96 litre unit with a bore of 3¾ in. and a stroke of 5½ in. The transmission was, however, the same as for the PLSC1. The rear axle was different, being worm driven. Devon General tried out six of these with Hall Lewis 26-seat dual entrance/exit coach bodies (Nos. 118–23), and Keighley Corporation used their half-dozen (Nos. 43–8) as 26-seater buses.

In 1929 the Lioness underwent a radical change becoming, in effect, a 6 cylinder version of the Lion LT1. Its designation was altered to LTB1. It was sometimes called the Lioness 6 to denote its variation from the 4 cylindered PLC1 model. The LTB1 lasted until 1933, after which it was withdrawn from production, presumably since it found so few customers. One of its principal patrons was Southdown, who equipped their first touring coach fleet with LTB1s bearing 20-seat luxury bodies built by Harrington. Numbered at first 301–17, they were later modernised and did not end their cruises to the West Country and the Trossacks until 1952.

## Leyland Tiger. Pl. 140–143

At the 1927 Commercial Motor Show the Leyland Tiger appeared as the single-deck counterpart ot the Titan and in its T type engine, brakes, chassis design, and so on, it was almost identical to the double-decker. By 1930 three versions of the Tiger were being marketed these differing in their dimensions as follows:—

| Model | Wheelbase | Overall Length |
|-------|-----------|----------------|
| TS1 | 17 ft 6 ins. | 27 ft. 6 ins. |
| TS2 | 17 ft. 6 ins. | 26 ft. |
| TS3 | 16 ft. 6 ins. | 26 ft. |

Dundee Corporation patronised the TS1 by buying a pair fitted with 31-seat rear entrance Dickson bus bodies. (Nos. 29/31, TS 9114/3). Black & White bought two batches of the TS2 and had 26-seat front entrance bodies made by London Lorries (Nos. 22–39 and 51–60); Southdown began their '1000' series of express coaches with a similar nine vehicles, but with rear entrances. G.S.R. bought seven and fitted to the chassis their own 32-seat bus bodies (Nos. TP 1–4 and OTP 1–3). Meanwhile, the Londonderry Lough Swilly Railway purchased a trio of TS3s equipped with 31-seat front entrance Catherwood bus bodies (Nos. 7, 35 and 36).

During the period 1933–5 the newly formed London Passenger Transport Board acquired forty early Tigers to form their TR class. Half of these came from Premier Line Ltd., and most of them were repainted in Green Line Livery. The next, most important source of Tigers for the L.P.T.B. was Maidstone & District with thirteen vehicles.

In 1932 the equivalent of the Titan TD2 was the Tiger TS4 with its fully-floating rear axles and servo-brakes, together with a more powerful 7·6 litre engine. At the same time the dimensions of the TS4 were the same as the older TS1. Oil engines were fitted to some TS4s. In 1933 this model was superseded by the TS6, which like its companion from the Leyland stable, the TD3, had a redesigned front which resulted in the

saving of bonnet space, and an increase in the area available for passengers.

The introduction of the hydraulic master cylinder attached to a vacuum-hydraulic braking system meant that the Tiger was once more altered to the TS7 model. Some TS7s were designated as TS7c, since they had torque converters like their Titan contemporaries. Sheffield Corporation had some of these with 32-seat rear entrance Craven bus bodies (Nos. 87–9, BWB 87–9; 183–203, BWB 183, etc.). Another version had a second trailing axle fitted to the rear of the vehicle so that it could meet Ministry of Transport requirements for 30 ft. long vehicles. City Coach Company bought eighteen of this TS7T (T for Trailing) model in 1935–6 as their Nos. LT1–18. Some had 39-seat bodies and others sat 43 passengers. This operator had an equal number of the rarer TS7D (D for Driven rear axle), which appeared outwardly to be identical. Nos. LT19–36 (CYO 191—6/DUC 901–12) all sat 43 people and had central entrances. Southdown had a pair of TS6Ts (Nos. 50/1, AUF 850/1) and a pair of TS7Ts (Nos. 52/3, BUF 552/3).

At the Commercial Motor Show for 1937 the TS8 made its debut. Like the TD5, this only varied from its immediate predecessors by such items as redesigned dumb-irons. Once again Sheffield took into its ranks a number of 'gearless' TS8cs with a variety of fleet numbers during 1937 and 1939. Bolton Corporation also tried out a quartet of this type (Nos. 1–4, ABN 401–4) with 32-seat Park Royal bodies.

No TS9 or TS10 models were ever built, but in 1937 the FEC version of the Tiger with an underfloor engine was supplied to London Transport as their TF1 (DYL 904). The engine in question was a Leyland 8·6 litre oil unit developing 94 b.h.p. and it was situated behind the driver's cab on the offside. The radiator sloped down from the front bulkhead to the headlamp on the front nearside wing, and gave the bus a most unusual appearance. Transmission was through a fluid flywheel and a compressed air driven pre-selective gearbox in the remainder of the TF class which entered service during 1939, but, in TF1, it was by means of an electro-pneumatically operated gearbox and single rear wheels. TF2–13 (FJJ 603–14) had 33-seat front entrance Park Royal bus bodies, but all but TF9 were destroyed in an air raid on Bull Yard, Peckham in October 1940. TF14–88 (FJJ 615–74/761–77/FXT 41–8) had London Transport built 34-seat bodies and spent much of their time working Green Line routes 712, 713, 714, 723 and 727.

It was not until 1941 that the final version of the TS series of the Tiger began to come off the production line. The TS11 had fully flexible engine mountings, being the single-deck form of the TD7. D.U.T. bought some as their R 243–6 (ZD 926–9) in 1944 and built their own 62-seat double-deck bodies on them! This was not, however, the first time that a Tiger had been double-decked as in the previous year Birch Bros. had replaced the single-deck body on their K51 (CYY 192), a TS7T, and built their own 54-seat double-deck body instead, renumbering it K 151.

Most of the TS11 chassis were 'frozen' by the government, and later allocated by them to those in need. Just over twenty chassis were involved and most of these went to independents, Yelloway of Rochdale getting the most, a trio EDK 726/40/2, which received 35-seat bus bodies from Burlingham.

In 1936 Leylands produced a few normal control Tigers with large bonnets and these were know as Tigresses. No designation was given to this chassis, however. Southdown took six of them and had Nos. 318–23 (CUF 318–23) fitted with luxurious Burlingham bodies seating only 20 and with central entrances.

Devon General took ten (Nos. 336–45, AOD 599–608) and equipped them with 26-seat front entrance Harrington bodies, again for coach duties only.

**Leyland Cub.** Pl. 131, 132
It was at their Kingston-on-Thames factory in 1932 that Leylands began to build their first lightweight Cubs. To power these vehicles a 4·4 litre 6 cylinder petrol engine with a bore of $3\frac{3}{8}$ in. and a stroke of 5 in. was specially constructed. This was the first Leyland unit since 1925 to have side valves. The Cub had many of the features, however, of the larger Tiger and Titan range such as fully floating rear axle, but with such a small vehicle only hydraulic brakes were deemed to be necessary. The Cub was designated KP (i.e. K type Passenger) and another version with forward control in place of normal control was given the prefix S for Side-type. The wheelbase and therefore the seating capacity of these early models of the Cub varied considerably, viz.:

| Model | Wheelbase | Seats |
|-------|-----------|-------|
| KP2 | 14 ft. 0 ins. | 20 |
| KP3 | 15 ft. 6 ins. | 24 |
| KP4 | 13 ft. 0 ins. | 14 |
| SKP3 | 15 ft. 6 ins. | 26 |

Whereas Devon General's solitary KP2 (No. 103, AUO 512) had a Mumford 20-seat body, Southdown's pair (Nos. 1/2, ACD 101/2) had Harrington coach bodywork with canvas roofs which sat a mere 14 passengers. Nowadays, we think of Black & White having large capacity coaches but, back in 1933, their Nos. 70–73 (DG 6557–60) were of the KP3 model with 20-seat Duple bodies.

In 1935 two new engines appeared for the Cub. The Light Six petrol engine had a capacity of 4·7 litres, a bore of $3\frac{1}{2}$ in. and a stroke of 5 in. The oil version was similar in size and was of the indirect injection variety. This led to a redesignation of Cub types as below:—

| Old Designation | New Designation |
|---|---|
| KP2 | KPZ1 |
| KP3 | KPZ2 |
| SKP3 | SKPZ2 |

In 1939 the provision of vacuum-servo assistance to the brakes led to the KPZ1 becoming the KPZ3 and the KPZ2 the KPZ4. On the other hand the SKPZ2 was replaced in 1938 by the Cheetah LZ3 model.

Southdown continued to take into its fleet numbers of Cubs as both one-man-operated buses and as excursion coaches. The former had Park Royal bodies and the latter had them by Harringtons. Wilts & Dorset, who had tried out a brace of KP3s (Nos. 119/20, WV 7333/4) in 1935, bought a further two, this time KPZ2s (Nos. 146/7, AHR 521/2), the following year. Great Southern Railway built their own 20-seat *rear* entrance bodies for two batches of KPZ1s delivered in 1936 (ZA 9324-7/9436-8). Among municipalities Coventry purchased three KPZ2s with 20-seat Brush bus bodies in 1936 (Nos. 143-5, BDU 143/4 and BHP 145). During 1935 and 1936 London Transport took into its ranks 20-seat Cubs for both central and country, lightly trafficked routes, with bodywork by Short (Nos. C 2-76, BXD 626-700) and Weymann (Nos. C77-98, CLE 105-26). Later for the inter-termini routes in central London a further batch with 18-seat, half-deck bodies built by Park Royal were bought as Nos. C106-113 (CLX 543-50). C1 (AYV 717) came in 1934, and its Leyland engine was later replaced by a Perkins unit. London Transport later took some unusual Cubs with rear mounted oil engines to form their CR class. The prototype (CR1, ELP 294) arrived in 1938, but the outbreak of war prevented the completion in 1939 of the building of CR2-60 (FXT 108-66), which

therefore stopped short at CR49. CR1 had a body constructed at the L.P.T.B's own works at Chiswick and had a direct injection diesel unit.

## Leyland Cheetah. Pl. 35
The Commercial Motor Show of 1935 saw the debut of yet another member of the Leyland Zoo. The Cheetah was definitely a hybrid, being part Lion, part Cub with a few pedigree parts added as the following table demonstrates:—

| Cub assemblies | Lion assemblies | Original |
|---|---|---|
| stub axle | radiator | frame |
| wheels | bonnet | front axle beam |
| hubs | steering | |
| clutch | column | |
| gearbox | front end | |
| rear axle | | |
| brakes | | |

Added to the original pair of models (LZ1 and LZ2) differing only in wheelbases, the LZ3 was added in 1937 as a replacement for the forward control Cub (the SKPZ2 model). At the same date vacuum hydraulic brakes were made an alternative as the table below shows. Further braking improvements turned the LZ3 into the LZ4, and the LZ2A into the LZ5 in 1938. All Cheetahs were powered by the Leyland Light Six 4·7 litre engine, which came in both petrol and oil versions.

| Model | Wheelbase | Brakes |
|---|---|---|
| LZ1 | 16 ft. 9 ins. | Hydraulic |
| LZ2 | 17 ft. 7 ins. | Hydraulic |
| LZ2A | 17 ft. 7 ins. | Vacuum-hydraulic |
| LZ3 | 15 ft. 6 ins. | Vacuum-hydraulic |
| LZ4 | 15 ft. 6 ins. | Vacuum-hydraulic |
| LZ5 | 17 ft. 7 ins. | Vacuum-hydraulic |

The largest operator of Cheetahs was Ribble who, during the period of 1936-9, bought 237 of this type, using them both as coaches and as service buses. In Hampshire, Southdown based their LZ3s (Nos. 500-4, EUF 500-4) and

LZ4s (Nos. 505–10, FUF 505–10) at their Hayling Island garage. Their Park Royal 24-seat, central entrance coach bodies provided suitably light coaches and relief buses for negotiating the rather shaky old road bridge that joined Hayling to the mainland at Langstone. Nearby Portsmouth Corporation also operated half a dozen LZ4s (Nos. 41–6, BTP 941–6), which had locally built Wadham 32-seat, rear entrance bus bodies. In the Channel Islands J.M.T. purchased a pair with Thurgood 26-seat rear entrance coach bodies in 1937 (Nos. C3/4, J 10244/5).

## Leyland Gnu

In 1937 Alexander took delivery of a most unusual vehicle as their No. P411 (WG 6608). This was the prototype Leyland Gnu TEP1. This had twin steering axles at the front and was powered by a Leyland 8·6 litre oil engine, the transmission being by means of a 4 speed gearbox and a single-plate clutch. The wheelbase was 16 ft. 3 ins. and Alexanders' own 40-seat body was 30 ft. in length. The following year a second TEP1 entered the Alexander fleet (P436, WG 6676). Meanwhile, the City Coach Company had taken the third Gnu of this model to come out of Leyland's factory as their G1 (FGC 593). This had a 40-seat Duple coach body. Whereas this vehicle had a central entrance the Alexander ones had front entrances.

In 1939 City Coach Company took the only five Gnu TEC2s ever assembled as their G2–6 (HVW 213–17). These differed from the TEP1s by having centrally mounted radiators instead of offset ones. The Duple bodies supplied, this time seated 39. They were used on the operator's Southend–Wood Green express service.

In 1940 Alexander bought the only Leyland Panda to be built and numbered it P683 (WG 9519). They gave it a 45-

seat body. In most respects the Panda was a development of the Gnu but it had an underfloor positioned engine.

## Maudslay CP Series

The Maudslay seven ton chassis could be used for both heavy lorries and for double-decked buses. In the latter form it had overhead worm drive for the rear axle, as in the case of Coventry Corporation's No. 12 (HP 5744) supplied in 1923, complete with a 58-seat open top Hickman body. There followed two more of this combination in 1924 (Nos. 13/4, HP 9001/2) and a further pair the following year (Nos. 15/6, RW 1999/8). However, at the 1925 Olympia Show Maudslay introduced a low level frame version of the CP with a wheelbase of 15 ft. 10 in., which was suitable for 54-seat double-decked work. The four cylinder engine developed 72 b.h.p. Again Coventry purchased some of these new CPs. Nos. 17–19 (RW 5001/2/119) had 54-seat Hickman bodywork with roofed in upper saloons, but retaining open staircases. This 7·0 litre engine (bore 4¾ in.; stroke 6 in.) had an underslung worm drive to the rear axle. Because of the lowering of the chassis this revised model was designated as the CPL.

There was a further modernisation of this chassis in 1929, when it became the CPL2 (or Magna, a name later used for the six wheeled version of the ML7). Once again Coventry liked the Maudslay double-decker and their Nos. 36–9 (WK 7686–9) received 48-seat Vickers bodywork, this time with enclosed staircases.

## Maudslay ML Series Pl. 36

It was in the autumn of 1924 that Maudslay of Alcester introduced their ML series of chassis. They were all powered by Maudslay o.h.c. engines of various sizes. The smallest was a four cylinder 4·06 litre unit with a bore of 100 mm and a stroke of 130 mm, and the larger engine, by having its bore increased to 110 mm, had a capacity of 4·94 litres. The engine and the gearbox were mounted in a subframe, which, by having a downward inclination, enabled a straight transmission line to the underslung worm-driven rear axle. Four wheel brakes were provided.

The following table summarises the main differences between the original members of the ML family.

| Model | Wheelbase | Control | Bore (mm) | Seats |
|-------|-----------|---------|-----------|-------|
| ML2/22 | 15 ft. 0 in. | Normal | 100 | 22 |
| ML3/35 | 16 ft. 6 ins. | Forward | 110 | 35 |
| ML4/26 | 15 ft. 2 ins. | Normal | 100 | 26 |
| ML4/30 | 16 ft. 8 ins. | Normal | 100 | 30 |
| ML4/30/110 | 16 ft. 8 ins. | Normal | 110 | 30 |

In 1932–3 the ML3 began to be called the Masta and the title Montrose was given to the ML4. By that date the ML2 had ceased to be built.

For the 1927 Olympia a 6 cylinder version, the ML6, was given its debut. This was driven by a 7·4 litre unit with bore/stroke measurements of 110 mm/130 mm. Transmission was via a single plate clutch and a 4 speed sliding mesh gearbox. Dewandre servo devices were fitted to the braking system. Wheelbase dimensions of 16 ft. 8 ins. ensured a 26 ft. overall body length for the ML6, but, at a later stage, some received 27 ft. 6 ins. bodywork. The name Meteor was allotted to this particular model in the early 'thirties.

Finally, in 1930, Maudslays brought out their double-deck form of this chassis, the ML7 (alias the Mentor), which had a 16 ft 6 ins. wheelbase. In 1931 a six-wheeled version of the ML7 (the Magna) arrived on the scene with a wheelbase of 16 ft. 2 ins. (measured to the centre of the rear bogie).

Who purchased all these chassis? One of their most faithful clients was George Ewer, who, since the late 'twenties, has been running express services from North London to most of the usual seaside resorts frequented by cockneys. The first pair of ML4/26s arrived early in 1927 (YE 8767/8), followed quickly by a further brace (YF 1030/1). In 1928 Ewer began to give all new coaches names, and so his next couple of ML4/26 coaches entered the fleet as 'Finsbury' (UC 7161) and 'Kingsland' (UC 7162). A slightly larger ML4 (sometimes called the ML4B, i.e. ML4/30) was also purchased in the shape of 'Britannia' (YV 6871), 'Olympia' (YV 6872), 'Majestic' (YV 8649) and 'The Homeric' (YW 4088). Late in 1928, among the next batch of ML4s (UL 1811–4), came their first ML3 (UL 1810), 'Resplendent'. It seems rather ironic that their first ML6 was given the name 'Invisible' (UU 1548)! In 1936 Ewers were still patronising Maudslays since in that year they bought CXL 652–4, a trio of the latest ML5s. This model was an improved version of the ML3, with a wheelbase of 17 ft. 7½ ins. These were, in fact, the last Maudslays to enter this fleet. Coming in the opposite direction, from Coast to Metropolis, were the Maudslays of Fairways of Worthing. They had 24-seat Dodson bodywork fitted to their ML3s, UL 1509 and UL 8823/4, and shortly afterwards they invested in a pair of ML4s, GU 8930/1. Other MLs operated by this express coach firm were registered as YX 3815, YX 5346, YW 9699 and YW 9762. These had bodies by Elliotts of Reading.

Among municipalities, Exeter during the period 1929–31, bought several ML3s and these received 32- or 31-seat dual entrance/exit Northern Counties bodywork for bus duties within that city (Nos. 5–14). Coventry Corporation purchased a series of ML4s equipped with Hickman 26-seat dual entrance/exit bodies between 1927 and 1929 (Nos. 20–35) and Dundee Corporation tried out two of the ML6s with 31-seat rear entrance Dickson bodywork in 1931 (Nos. 33/4, TS 9115/6). In 1929 Coventry took delivery of seventeen ML7 six-wheelers with Brush bodywork and three similarly bodied four-wheelers.

As from 1937 the ML5 became known as the Marathon and, as an alternative, a Gardner 4LW or 5LW oil engine could be fitted instead of the 5·43 litre Maudslay petrol engine.

## Maudslay SF40

1935 brought onto the market a 40-seater with a fully fronted appearance which was at first termed merely the SF40 (i.e. Single-deck Fully-fronted 40-seater). It was well ahead of its time through having the front axle sufficiently far back to allow a truly forward entrance. Its maximum overall length was 27 ft. 6 ins. The wheelbase was understandably reduced to 15 ft. Triple servo brakes were fitted. The engine was a 4 cylinder 5·34 litre petrol unit but, as from 1937, an option was available in the form of the Gardner 4LW and 5LW diesel engine. By that date the SF40 had become the third holder of the popular Maudslay name of Magna. Another Midlands firm, Willow-brook of Loughborough, fitted many of the bodies such as that on Blackheath & District's No. 10 (APT 141), but we do find an unusual Holbrook coach body on AUY 155, belonging to Johnson of Stourbridge, and Ledgard's CUB 1 had a 36-seat *central* entrance Brush coach body. Stevenson of Uttoxeter called for a 40-seat dual purpose body from Burling-hams, for their No. 11 (CRE 13) in 1935.

## N.G.T. SE6

It was in 1933 that Mr. G. W. Hayter, the Chief Engineer of Northern General Transport, decided to design his own single-decker for the company, using the space available more economically. The result was the SE6, standing for Side-Engined six-wheeler. The prototype, No. 586 (CN 5674), was 30 ft. long,

which meant that, under Ministry regulations, it had to have a third axle, which, in the case of the SE6, was in the form of a trailing one at the rear. The main problem was in finding a suitable petrol engine that could not only power a comparatively large vehicle but also fit into the restricted space available. The answer was found in an American unit, the Hercules WXRT 6 cylinder engine, with a swept volume of 6·3 litres, a bore of $4\frac{1}{4}$ in. and a stroke of $4\frac{1}{2}$ in. An American built Fuller gearbox was also used. The final drive assembly was of N.G.T. design. The chassis frame was unusual through having equidistant side members throughout its length. Short Bros. fitted a 45-seat body to the first SE6 with an entrance just to the rear of the front axle. A further quintet appeared in 1934 as Nos. 604–8 (CN 6100–4) with wheelbases of 16 ft. $7\frac{1}{2}$ ins. dimension.

In 1935 the production of the SE6 really got under way. There were some modifications such as the use of a David Brown gearbox that had helical gears in constant mesh for the second and third gears, which helped to make the SE6 a relatively silent bus to operate. Vacuum-hydraulic brakes were fitted and flexible engine mountings assisted in making it a modern vehicle. Once again Short Bros. built the single-deck bus bodies, but now the entrance was placed forward of the front axle. Northern General itself took delivery of Nos. 657–75 (CN 6616–34) and its subsidiary, Tynemouth & District Transport Company, took Nos. 82–6 (FT 3478–82). At the same time N.G.T. had others (Nos. 651–6, CN 6610–5) fitted with 28-seat luxury coach bodies for tourist duties. One extra vehicle (N.G.T. No. 676, CN 6635) was given a Weymann 45-seat bus body. The coaches needed an even more powerful engine and so they received the Hercules WXLC3 unit of 6·65 litres, with a bore of $4\frac{1}{4}$ in. and a stroke of $4\frac{3}{4}$ in.

The final batch of SE6s were built during 1936 and consisted of N.G.T. Nos. 727/8 (CN 7430/1), with Beadle built 28-seat touring bodies, and Tynemouth Nos. 90–2 (FT 3903–5), with Weymann 44-seat bus bodies. Between 1943 and 1947 all but the prototype SE6 and the coaches were given oil engines in the form of the A.E.C. 184 engines removed from Matilda tanks. At the same time Ministry approval was given for the removal of the trailing axle, thus converting them in reality to SE4s.

### N.G.T. SE4
In 1936 Northern General experimented with a two axle version of their successful side-engined six-wheeler. No. 701 (AUP 590) had an English Electric 40-seat body with the entrance forward of the front axle. This proved to be much lighter, and therefore more economical, than the SE6.

When the SE4 went into production later, in 1938, it was fitted with a diesel engine in place of the American petrol unit. The engine selected was the A.E.C. A172 indirect injection Ricardo type, of 6·75 litres swept volume, and with bore and stroke of 105 mm and 130 mm respectively. The engine was accommodated by inclining the cylinders. N.G.T. Nos. 802–26 (CPT 902–26) were given similar English Electric bodies to the prototype. The SE4 had an overall length of 27 ft. 6 ins.

### Railless
One of the oldest names in the manufacture of trolleybuses is that of Railless, a branch of Short Bros. of Rochester and Bedford. The first four single-deckers placed into service by York Corporation in 1920 were of this make. Birmingham Corporation purchased a dozen of this make for their first essay into trolleybus operation on the Nechells route in 1922. Nos. 1–12 (OK 4823–34) had Roe, 51-

seat bodies which had roofs on their upper decks, but which retained the open staircases. Indeed, trolleybuses were provided with such cover by some operators before the motorbuses in their fleets achieved that degree of civilization. In 1923 Ipswich Corporation had bought three of the single-deck version. Nos. 1–3 (DX 3920, 3988 and 3906) also had Railless bodies seating 30 passengers and provided with central entrances. An open top Railless was supplied to West Hartlepool Corporation the following year.

At the 1925 Commercial Motor Show Railless displayed three trolleybuses. One was a 37-seat single-decker, one was a 51-seat highbridge double-decker and the third was a new model seating 52. This latter had a low ground clearance for a trolleybus of this period, 2 ft 8½ ins., which gave a total height from the road surface of 14 ft. 6 ins. It was powered by two English Electric 35 h.p. motors.

In 1925 Ashton-under-Lyne Corporation started off their trolleybus fleet with eight Railless single-deckers. Nos. 50–57 were powered by pairs of English Electric 99A motors of 35 h.p. and were given 36-seat central entrance bodies by Short Bros. (alias Railless). The last Railless trolleybuses were bought by Nottingham Corporation in 1927 as their Nos. 1–10 (TO 5002–11). It is rather strange that so many operators made their initial choice Railless, and yet switched to other makes for subsequent batches of vehicles. If Railless were so unreliable one would have thought word would be quickly spread to prevent such original purchases occurring.

### Ransomes, Sims & Jefferies Two Axle Trolleybus
It was in 1924 that the first R.S.J. trolleybus entered service, in its native Ipswich, as that Corporation's No. 4 (DX 3648) with a Ransomes single-deck dual entrance/exit body. From that

date nearly every purchase of trolleybuses in that Suffolk town consisted of repeat orders for R.S.J. four-wheelers, right up to the very last R.S.J. ever to be built, which became No. 86 (PV 6426) in 1940. By then, however, Ransomes had handed over the bodybuilding side to others, in this case to Masseys, who provided, for No. 86, a 48-seat double-deck rear entrance bus body. Altogether, Ipswich Corporation had R.S.J. trolleybuses filling fleet Nos. 4–20, 36–44 and 46–86, the gaps being early Railless's (Nos. 1–3) and Garretts (Nos. 21–35/45) vehicles. From No. 46 onwards were double-deckers. Another 'fan' of Ransomes, Sims & Jefferies, however, came from the other side of England, St. Helens Corporation. They started off their run of R.S.Js with a single-deck 32-seater with central entrance, in 1928. No. 5 (DJ 3684) had an R.S.J. motor, but English Electric equipment. There followed four 35-seaters of similar pattern the next year (Nos. 105–8, DJ 4081–4). After a lull of five years trolleybus expansion led to the first of a series of 50-seat lowbridge double-deckers. Nos. 116–20 (DJ 6051–4) had Brush bodywork and Nos. 137–41 (DJ 6863–7) 142–4 (DJ 7236–8) and 145–56 (DJ, 8120–31) not only had Massey bodies but also Crompton Parkinson–Allan West equipment.

Other municipalities 'flirted' with R.S.J. from time-to-time. Such a one was Rotherham with their 32-seat single-deckers, ET 3217 and 4818–20, powered by R.S.J. 60 h.p. motors. Darlington in 1928 had two similar vehicles (Nos. 25/6, HN 6204/3). Both Derby in 1932 (No. 101, RC 801 with an R.S.J. 56-seat highbridge body) and Reading in 1936 (No. 5, RD 8089 with a Park Royal 52-seat lowbridge body) used a four-wheel R.S.J. in an experiment with other similar trolleybuses, but did not order any for their tram replacement programmes.

## Ransomes, Sims & Jefferies
## Three Axle Trolleybus

The need for a third axle for longer vehicles meant that, in common with most other trolleybus manufacturers, Ransomes, Sims & Jefferies found it necessary to offer a six-wheeler model. However, this did not seem to be as popular as their four-wheeler product. St. Helens Corporation did invest in a quintet of these in 1931 fitted with R.S.J. 60-seat lowbridge bodywork and with R.S.J. motors, but English Electric equipment. In 1928 Maidstone Corporation too, had tried out this larger R.S.J. and Nottingham Corporation in the early days of its trolleybus system also tried out three axle electric vehicles.

## Reo Speedwagon

It was in 1924 that R. E. Olds of Oldsmobile, the big American car firm, began to flood the small independent operators' market with the first of his p.s.v. offerings, the Speedwagon. The 4 cylinder FB model was cheap; in 1925 the chassis cost as little as £295, and yet it could seat 20 passengers. At first it was planned as a 14-seater, to be more or less a rival to that other trans-Atlantic success, the Model T Ford. TY 6926 was such a vehicle, but soon, in its larger form, it met the needs of many of the one-man country operators. The Speedwagon lasted in production to about 1931.

## Reo Sprinter. Pl. 149

The next expensive Reo model after the Speedwagon was the Sprinter at £320 in 1925. This was a 6 cylinder model and, presumably, its more powerful engine helped it to live up to its name, a name that would appeal to the often 'speed-crazy' so-called 'pirates', who were trying to steal custom from the longer established operators with their slower, larger buses.

Contemporary with the Sprinter was the refined Major with its 6 cylinder 24·3 h.p. engine, which developed 50 b.h.p. at 2,000 r.p.m. The Major had a wheelbase of 13 ft., an overall length of 18 ft. 10 ins. and a width of 5 ft. 6 ins. so that it could tackle the narrowest of rural routes. The transmission was through a multiple-disc clutch and a 3 speed gearbox, the final drive being via a spiral bevel. The Major was designed to cope with between 18 and 20 seats and it cost £475.

The dearest of this generation of Reos was the Pullman, as its title suggests. With single tyres at the rear it came to £570, but, with the safety of twin tyres it rose to £595. Powered by the same engine as the Major the GB (as the Pullman was designated) could carry up to 24 passengers. Black & White Motorways bought five Pullmans in 1928, Nos. 11–15 being given 20-seat London Lorries coach bodies. MY 4217 is an example with a 24-seat Strachans coach body.

### Reo Gold Crown

As from 1929 Reo concentrated on a new model, the Gold Crown. Most of these had 20-seat bodies. (e.g. VX 1072 with one by Bush & Twiddy; VX 1467 with one by Waveney), however, some Gold Crowns carried as many as 26 passengers in a bus form (e.g. TM 8402, of 1932 vintage).

### Saurer 3A Pl. 39

In 1925 a Swiss manufacturer, Saurer, began their run of success with the British market in the shape of their 3A model. This was a 40 h.p. vehicle with a bore/stroke of 110 mm/180 mm and it was planned as a 26-seater, its wheelbase being 15 ft. 6 ins. It had a low platform, this being 2 ft. 4 ins. from the road surface, when the vehicle was laden. An interesting feature is that its drive was completely enclosed.

At the next Olympia a larger 4BL model emerged from the Saurer stable.

This was a 6 cylinder version with bore/stroke of 110 mm/150 mm, which developed 105 b.h.p. at 1,600 r.p.m., a very good performance for this period. With a wheelbase of 19 ft. it could take a body of up to 29 ft. 6 ins. in length and 7 ft. 2½ ins. in width. The 4BL was lower than the 3A, being a mere 1 ft. 4½ ins. from the road.

A third Saurer to appear in this country was the small 2BH model, which was in reality a minibus. Thus, National Omnibus & Transport's No. 2851 (TW 4093) of 1926 had a 12-seat London Lorries body.

### Shelvoke & Drewry Freighter. Pl. 40–42

Although basically a chassis designed for use with municipal authorities as dustcarts, gully emptiers, and so on, the tenth chassis to be built, late in 1923, was fitted with an 18-seat front entrance bus body by Hickman and was used as a demonstrator. The first firm to take an interest in it was that of W. Gates of Worthing, who hoped to start a sea front route using a small vehicle, which would be sufficiently near the ground so as not to discourage the elderly residents from boarding it. Because the S.D. Freighter had a tram style controller lever for the gears to be operated by the driver's left hand and tiller steering by the right hand, Mr. Gates called his new service the Tram-O-Cars. The first vehicle, No. 1, (BP 9822) entered service in April 1924, and was soon followed by the demonstrator as No. 2 (PX 262). Instead of windows their bodies were fitted with roller blinds to be drawn down in the case of inclement weather. Another 1924 Freighter ended up, in 1926, with Price's Motors of Dinas Powis, Glamorganshire, who used this 20-seater on their Dinas Powis–Penarth route. TX 1506, in the following year, was bought by Mr. W. J. Abbott of Exmouth for his Withycombe–Exmouth–Orcombe Point run.

In 1925 Plymouth Corporation purchased a trio of Freighters fitted with 20-seat Hickman bodies (Nos. 22–4, CO 8190–92) for their circular route 22 round the Hoe area. The following season this corporation bought a further three and numbered them 45–7 (CO 9517–19). In 1925 Bournemouth Corporation took delivery of a brace of Freighters with 20-seat dual entrance/exit bodies built by Chalmers & Sons (RU 1814/5, later Nos. 7/8). These were to replace the 16-seater Guy Run-abouts which had been employed since 1923 on the undercliff route between Bournemouth Pier and Boscombe Pier. In 1926 a further four Freighters arrived to augment this service, namely, RU 2266–9 (later numbered 9–12. The third municipality to buy p.s.v. Freighters was Blackpool, who needed them for a route between Adelaide Street and Forest Gate. These four had 24-seat toastrack bodies built by Shelvoke & Drewry themselves (Nos. 35–8, FR 7452–5). The only other municipality to purchase a Freighter was Belfast, who used their 1930 vintage No. 6 (AZ 5450) on the steep 1 in 5 road from Antrim Road up to the Pleasure Garden on the plateau. This vehicle had a 28-seat toastrack body built by William Derby & Sons of Belfast.

The other main concentration of Freighters occurred in North Wales, where White Rose of Rhyl (alias Brookes Bros.) bought their first one in 1926. DM 4833 (No. 54) was given a toastrack body by Simpson & Slater with 32 seats. No. 64 (DM 5266) followed in 1928, and then, in 1929, came another trio (Nos. 71–73, DM 6233–5). Before taking up their duties at Rhyl, they had been used for internal transport at the 1929 Wembley Exhibition, being called 'Raildok' cars there. After Brookes Bros. sold out to Crosville, the latter bought further Freighters and introduced them to visitors at other Welsh resorts such as Barmouth

and Aberystwyth. These further batches were delivered in 1931 (Nos. 626–8, FM 6459–61), 1935 (U18–21, FM 9063–6) and 1937 (U12–14, CFM 340–2). The latter had 32-seat toastrack bodies built by Eastern Coachworks. Eventually, Tram-O-Cars built up a fleet of a dozen Freighters and after they were acquired by Southdown in 1938 the only two rear engined Freighters (T16/7, FCD 16/7) with Harrington 26-seat central entrance bodies entered service. In Jersey, General Service Garages of St Helier bought four in 1932 from Blackpool Corporation and these were re-registered as J 6420, J 6473, J 7196 and J 7419. J.M.T. purchased the first two Freighters manufactured from Worthing, and ran them as their Nos. 22/3 (J 7854/5).

The engine in the original Freighters was only 13 b.p.h. but, in 1928, a slightly more powerful unit developing 16 b.p.h. was substituted. This ran at up to 3,000 r.p.m. In 1929 the wheelbase was lengthened from 11 ft. up to 13 ft 3 ins. The engine was again improved in 1932 when it was uprated to 24 b.h.p. The bore of this unit was 80 mm and the stroke 120 mm, the final drive being through overhead worm. In 1933 Ministry of Transport regulations affected the Freighter design and wheel steering replaced the tiller. After 1928 most Freighters were fitted with pneumatic tyres in place of the former solids, but the diameter of the actual wheels still remains very small compared with other buses on the roads.

## S.M.C. Sikh

In 1928 the Sunbeam Motor Company entered the field of bus building by putting on sale their Sikh double-decker. This was a six-wheeler with a wheelbase of 18 ft. 6 ins. and an overall body length of 29 ft., thus enabling a 70-seat body to be fitted. It was powered by a Sunbeam 70/142 6 cylinder engine of

7·98 litres, which developed 142 b.h.p. at 2,400 r.p.m. Transmission was through a single plate clutch and a 4 speed constant mesh gearbox to an underslung worm rear axle. The demonstrator, UK 7456, had a rear entrance 67-seat body when built in 1929. After various trials, it was eventually bought by Derby Corporation in 1933. In 1930 the Westminster Omnibus Company bought a Sikh and had it given a Dodson 64-seat body. This London independent bought a second Sikh in 1933. Due to the quality of the Sikh, it was really non-competitive, and as such was a non-starter.

## S.M.C. Pathan

The S.M.C. Pathan was the single-deck equivalent. This had four wheels and was powered by a Sunbeam 52/110 engine. This 6 cylinder 6·6 litre unit developed 110 b.h.p. at 2,400 r.p.m. Transmission was the same as that working in the Sikh. The wheelbase was 16 ft. 6 ins. Only twenty-five Pathans were ever built, and three of these went to Wolverhampton Corporation as might have been expected. No. 87 (UK 8141) had a rare Rushton & Wilson 32-seat rear entrance body and Nos. 88/9 (UK 9488/9) had 31-seat Taylor bodywork. Other purchases included Red Garages of Llandudno and S.M.T. J. Stevenson of Spath, near Uttoxeter, Staffs. purchased one of the first and last Pathans. RF 7352 came in 1930 and CRF 349 arrived four years later. Both had Burlingham coach bodies seating 32, although, whereas the earlier vehicle had a front entrance, the later had a rear entrance.

## S.O.S. S Series

In 1923 the Chief Engineer of the Birmingham & Midland Motor Omnibus Company (known universally as 'Midland Red'), Mr. L. G. Wyndham Shire, designed, for B.M.M.O., the first of a series of single-deck chassis under the initials S.O.S. (standing for Shire's Own

Specifications). This prototype was designated the 'S' and was given a 4·344 litre 4 cylinder petrol engine with a bore of 4·134 in. and a stroke of 4·939 in. It had a 4 speed gearbox and was fitted with the then new (as far as buses were concerned) feature of pneumatic tyres. The first vehicle was HA 2330, which had a 32-seat front entrance Brush body as had the second prototype HA 2333. On the other hand, HA 2348 was given a 32-seat charabanc body by Davidsons. Altogether during that first year, sixteen buses (HA 2334–47 were the others) and six charabancs (HA 2348–53) appeared on the road. Of the fifty-six S type buses built in 1924, twenty-two were sold to other operators: Potteries Electric Traction, EH 4940–4/5149–53/5606 Peterborough Electric Traction, FL 3948/9/51–4; Llandudno Coaching & Carriage, CC 4537/9/4816 and Northern General Transport, PT 3422. On the other hand, only Potteries bought a Davidson bodied charabanc (EH 5148). By the time that the S ceased production in 1927, a grand total of 356 had been built, all but twenty being in bus form.

The S was a normal control model, but, in 1925, the S.O.S. forward control FS prototype was constructed with a 34-seat forward entrance Carlyle body, and this became the new shape for Midland Red and its associates for the best part of the next decade. HA 2500, like the S models, had that distinctive 'porch' over the doorway which was to become a recognisable feature on hundreds of ensuing buses. During 1926 a total of eighty-four FS chassis came off the assembly lines, all but eighteen of them being the bus version. Davidson's charabanc body also seated 34 passengers. The only two FS buses to be 'exported' went to Potteries as their Nos. 88/9 (EH 7901/2).

Eight years before A.E.C. used the letter Q for a chassis type, S.O.S. had adopted it, but then it stood for Quantity (of passengers). By lengthening the wheelbase from 15 ft. 7½ ins., shortening the bonnet and moving the driver forward, an extra three passengers could be seated. The prototype HA 3532, had a 37-seat front entrance body built by Midland Red's own Carlyle works. In 1927 two hundred Q buses were assembled, nearly half of them going to other operators. N.G.T. and Trent, with twenty-five apiece, took the lion's share.

Four smaller wheels to lower the height of the chassis introduced, in 1928, HA 3719, the first QL. For the first time an S.O.S. had all four wheels the same size. In the previous year HA 3666 had made the debut for the QC version, which was really the Q chassis with normal instead of forward control. The QC sat only 30 in charabanc style. Inside both the Q and the QL the saloon was divided into two compartments. The QL was a great success as far as production figures were concerned for no less than 349 were built, whereas the QC mustered only nineteen; perhaps a comment on the trend towards central gangwayed single-entrance coaches in place of the plank arrangements of the horse era. An attempt was made to modernise the QC by the same method that had turned the FS into the QL, by lowering, the chassis height from the ground. In this form the first QLC (HA 4824) appeared with a Short Bros. 29-seat charabanc body in 1928. Twenty-nine of this 4 cylinder model were produced (HA 4827 having a 6 cylinder unit) and then, in 1929, there came a similar sized batch of 6 cylinder engined QLCs, followed by a further 25 in 1929.

The QL had been tried in two cases with a new SS 6 cylinder engine of 5·047 litres, a bore of 3·8 in. and a stroke of 4·527 in. These were HA 4806 and HA 4809.

The next instalment of the S series came in 1929 when there appeared the first two M (for Madam) buses. HA 4907/8 were specially planned to win

over the women shoppers, by providing more space. Their Carlyle bodies seated 34. At the same time the partition between the two parts of the saloon was done away with. Following this brace came a further 165 M type buses, of which Northern General took delivery of forty, Trent of thirty, Potteries of twenty-five, Peterborough of twelve, Llandudno of six and Ortona (Camb.) of five.

## S.O.S. XL Series

The first real long distance express coaches to be operated and built by Midland Red were the XL class of 1929 HA 4956–99/ 5001–6 had 30-seat front entrance coach bodies built jointly by Brush and Carlyle. They were powered by the SS engine with its side valve, bore of 3·8 in. and stroke of 4·527 in. Its capacity was 5·047 litres and it was a 6 cylinder unit.

At the same time that Midland Red was developing its long distance coach routes it was also promoting a series of limited stop stage carriage routes, with an 'X' prefix to the route number. For this, a version of the XL, designated the COD, was built, with a 34-seat front entrance bus body by Carlyle. HA 5007 with its 6 cylinder SS unit went into service in 1930, and was followed by a further twenty-two buses, but with 4 cylinder engines and Brush bodywork (HA 5124, HA 6153–73). Potteries were also interested in the COD and bought twenty-one of them as their Nos. 201–21 (VT 4501–21) with Brush bodies. Trent too bought seventeen CODs.

The normal stage carriage bus at this time was the MM (Modernised Madam), which was basically the M with a re-styled 34-seat Ransomes body. Thirty-nine of these were supplied with 4 cylinder engines (one of which went to Trent) and were followed in 1930 by another ten with 6 cylinder units.

The next step in the development of the Madam was the IM4 (the I standing for Improved). Like the MM it was a restyling of the bodywork and in this case of the radiator as well. The prototype (HA 5085) had a 34-seat Carlyle body and came onto the road in 1930. A second prototype (HA 6226) was given a similar capacity Short Bros. body. This was the builder chosen for the first fifty production buses (HA 6176–225) of 1931. Two more went to Northern General and Trent as CN 4736 and CH 9916 respectively. Further IM4s were built the next year, but this time HA 8246–95 were fitted with bodies by either Brush or Metro-Cammell. The final batch for Midland Red were produced in 1933–4 with Short Bros. bodywork (HA 8324/5, HA 8348–57, HA 9358–75). Trent received 25 IM4s in both 1931 and 1932, and Potteries 6 in 1932.

A 6 cylinder version of the IM appeared in 1931. HA 6227–45 had 34-seat Brush bodies, which had been removed from earlier COD buses. Altogether, fifty of the IM6 entered the ranks of B.M.M.O. and Trent took a further twenty-six. Others found homes with Northern General (twenty) and its subsidiaries, Sunderland District (four) and Wakefield's Motors (two).

## S.O.S. RR Series

In 1930 the fifty XL coaches had their bodies removed and fitted onto new RR chassis, which used the new RR2 S.B. engine of 5·986 litres, with a bore of 3·938 in. and a stroke of 5 in. Later that year HA 6174 and HA 6175 arrived with new 30-seat Short Bros. front entrance coach bodies as the SRR class. A further ten SRRs went to N.G.T. Another version was the BRR (Bus RR), of which the first (HA 5123) had a 34-seat dual purpose Carlyle body. In 1934 twenty BRR chassis bearing Short Bros. 34-seat bus bodies entered service as HA 9376–95.

The next generation of Midland Red coaches started with the debut of the

LRR (HA 9051) in 1933, with its 30-seat front entrance Short Bros. body. As with the QL, the L meant Lower chassis. Although the same engine used in earlier members of the RR family was kept, a double-deck type of underslung worm driven rear axle was provided. In 1943 six LRRs with the same specifications as the prototype were manufactured, one of which went to P.M.T. (No. 247, AVT 567). In 1941 HA 9396–9400 were converted to 34-seat buses, since they were then redundant as coaches, due to wartime conditions. A further batch, of 1935 vintage, (AHA 587–611), met a similar fate during the Second World War.

AHA 612–36 introduced the OLR class of coaches with their Short Bros. 29-seat bodies with forward entrances. These were of normal control and had a wheelbase of 17 ft. 6 ins. Their size necessitated the use of the more powerful RR2 L.B. unit of 6·373 litres. During the Second World War they were converted not only to buses, like the LRR class, but also to forward control.

In 1937 came the SLR, which was really a forward control version of the OLR. The 30-seat English Electric bodies of CHA 950–99 were fully-fronted and had a slight rise in the floor level towards the rear of the saloon, for better observation on long cruises. Between 1938 and 1941 CHA 969 bore the prototype B.M.M.O. K oil engine. During 1947/8 the petrol engines were replaced by Leyland diesel units.

## S.O.S. ON Series. Pl. 151, 152

Fitted with Midland Red's new 5·986 litre 6 cylinder petrol engine, came the ON in 1934. It was equipped with the 'silent third' gearbox as had been its predecessor the IM6. Due to the legal overall length going up to 27 ft 6 ins. it was possible to extend the wheelbase to 17 ft. 6⅜ ins., thus giving room for 38 passengers. Indeed the Short Bros. bodies fitted to the HA 9451 class were a break with the style that had persisted for the previous decade and they had a much more modern appearance. Northern General (twelve), Sunderland District (ten) and Wakefields (two) purchased ON buses, but with only 32 seats. Trent took ten chassis, which were given Duple coach bodies of quite a different design. There were some variations within the ranks of those that worked for Midland Red. For instance, HA 9486 was designated to receive a special light-weight chassis as an experiment. HA 9457, instead of the Midland Red petrol unit, was tried out during its first year with a Dorman 4 cylinder oil engine and HA 9481/2/5 were a trio powered by the A.E.C. A171 diesel engine and therefore classified as DON vehicles (D for Diesel).

When a second batch were delivered during 1934-5 as AHA 487-536, AHA 523 for its first three years carried an experimental Clary oil engine. Trent took delivery of 6 ONs in 1935. The next group of DON buses had a mixture of Short Bros. and Brush bodywork (AHA 537-86), but one vehicle (AHA 541) until 1946 ran with a Gardner 5LW engine, and AHA 576 was the solitary petrol engined SON model. This had Cotal epicyclic gears. However, when the SON version went into full scale production in 1936, not only were English Electric asked to supply 39-seat bodies instead of Short Bros., but CHA 501-65 also had B.M.M.O K diesel engines as their power units. Further arrivals of SON/English Electric buses continued during 1937 (DHA 637-736) and 1938 (EHA 737-86), before a change was made, in 1939, to Brush bodywork, with FHA 449-86. The final production of SON/Brush 38-seaters occurred in 1940 when GHA 301-50 were built, making a grand total of 303 SON oil engined buses. Trent bought 30 DONs in 1935, 40 DONs and 6 ONs in 1936, 12 SONs in 1939 and 14 SONs in 1940.

During 1937-8 many of the ON buses

were given the K engine and thus became known as members of the new CON (Converted ON) class. In 1939 the last of the ON series appeared, the ONC (this time C stood for Coach). FHA 401-25 had 30-seat central entrance Duple bodywork. An Aphon gearbox with overdrive helped to cut the noise from the K engine. Until 1951 FHA 425 was called an LON (Luxury ON), being employed as the directors' coach. Trent purchased 6 ONC chassis.

## S.O.S. REDD

In 1932 Midland Red introduced their first home-built double-deck chassis called the REDD (for Rear Entrance Double-Decker). This had a wheelbase of 16 ft. 1½ ins. and carried a body with seats for 52 passengers (26 on each deck). It was powered by the Company's RR2 L.B. engine of 6.373 litres, with bore measurement of 4·062 in. and stroke of 5 in. dimension. This was a side valve 6 cylinder unit. A newly designed gearbox with helical gears gained the nick-name of 'the silent third', although this was rather a relative than an exact description. The rear axle was of the underslung worm type.

HA 7329, the prototype, had actually appeared on the scene a year before. Its 48-seat body, built by Short Bros., was different in appearance to the later REDD vehicles since the upper deck did not extend over the driver's cab, hence its reduced capacity. HA 8001-50 had a mixture of bodies constructed by Short Bros., Eastern Counties, Brush and Metro-Cammell. Potteries purchased four of this type (Nos. 27-30, VT 8601-4) which had lowbridge Brush bodies seating 52 passengers. Northern General took into their fleet what should have been HA 8002 in the B.M.M.O. fleet. Like the rest of that fifty its body was of the highbridge variety. Roller destination blinds were fitted, but the route numbers were in the form of a metal stencil.

## S.O.S. FEDD

1933 saw the debut of HA 9000, the first of a large number of double-deckers built by Midland Red before the outbreak of the Second World War. Naturally, the letters in its title spelt out Forward Entrance Double-Decker. This initial one of the series had a 52-seat Carlyle body but, when mass production began in the following year, the normal practice was to provide 56 seats. The first fifty (HA 9401–50) had Short Bros. bodies with 30 passengers on the top deck and 26 in the lower saloon. In 1935 eighty-five FEDDs came off the assembly line for Midland Red's own use. BHA 301–400 had Metro-Cammell bodywork, as did the 1936 smaller batch of BHA 801–35. A further half-century of FEDDs followed in 1938 with EHA 251–300, this time with Brush bodies, which were of composite construction. Three of these vehicles (EHA 290/2/7) were given full width cabs, although, two years later, they were converted to the half-cab appearance of the others. In 1942 another of this series (EHA 298) was given a so-called 'bull-nose' front, but this too, was given a more orthodox styling in 1951. During 1938–9 two further consignments of FEDDs entered service in the 'Black Country', again with 56-seat Brush bodywork. They were FHA 201–50 and FHA 836–85. Thus a total of 336 FEDDs were manufactured for 'internal consumption', a further 15 going to Trent. Other operators of S.O.S. double-deckers were now turning to other sources for their supplies. For example, after their last purchase of REDDs in 1934, (Nos, 232–46, AVT 552–66), P.M.T. turned to the Leyland Titan and the Daimler COG5 for their new double-deckers.

The FEDD had the same unit as the REDD, but the wheelbase was extended by 1¾ in. to 16 ft. 3¼ ins. Mr. Wyndham Shire realised that a more powerful oil engine was really needed for the FEDD and, eventually, he designed the K, (nicknamed 'kidney' engine, because of the shape of its combustion chamber), of 8·028 litres with a 4·45 in. bore and 5·25 in. stroke. It was a 6 cylinder direct injection unit. These were first fitted to the EHA batch. Beginning with the first FHA batch, German built ZF Aphon gearboxes were fitted, which extended the 'silent third' principle to the second gear as well. During 1937–8 some of the 1934 and 1935 FEDDs were re-equipped with K oil engines.

## Star Flyer. Pl. 43

In 1921 Star were advertising their 30 cwt. model with a wheelbase of 13 ft. 6 ins., along with a 3 Tonner which could seat 25 in a charabanc body. This had a 20–25 h.p. engine of 4 cylinders (90 mm/150 mm) and a worm drive to the rear axle.

By 1925 three wheelbase lengths were being offered by Star, 11 ft. (12–14 seats), 12 ft. (16–20 seats) and 13 ft. 6 ins. (20–25 seats).

Two years later the Star Flyer appeared with its 24 h.p. 6 cylinder o.h.v. engine (80 mm/120 mm). Transmission was through a double dry plate to a 4 speed gearbox and it could cope with 20 passengers. This must have been the VB4 model, one of which was purchased by Harper Bros. as their No. 2 (RF 3441) and fitted with a Bracebridge of Lincoln, 26-seat bus body with a front entrance. Two years later they bought a second VB4 identical to the first (No. 3, RF 6135). They also acquired VP 2891, a VB4 with a 20-seat Spicer body. Norfolk Motor Services had a 24-seat coach version of the VB4 in 1929 (EX 2294).

Black & White Motorways tried out a solitary VB6 in 1929. No. 40 (DF 8747) had a 26-seat London Lorries body.

Another variant was the VB3 of which UX 5054, with its 20-seat bus body of 1929 vintage, is an example.

## Straker-Clough Trackless

During the mid-'twenties Straker Squire and Clough Electrics combined to build trolleybuses in what looked like a very promising market. At the 1925 Show they exhibited two models. The 30-seat single-deck version had a wheelbase of 14 ft. 6 ins. and was powered by one motor. The 50-seat double-deck model had the same wheelbase, but needed a second motor to drive it efficiently.

In 1924 Keighley Corporation re-equipped its trolleybus fleet with vehicles of this make, starting off with four Dodson bodied single-deckers (Nos. 1–4, WT 6336/5/58/7). They were shortly followed by six Brush bodied double-deckers with open staircases (Nos. 5–10, WT 7101–6) and four more single-deckers, also with Brush bodywork and seating 32 passengers (Nos. 11–14, WT 7107–10). In the next year came a final quartet of Brush bodied double-deckers (Nos. 15–18, WU 2585–8). All had one or two, (according to size), British-Thompson-Houston K type motors.

1925 saw the commencement of the Darlington system with the arrival of twenty Roe bodied Straker-Cloughs seating 32 with a central entrance. Nos. 1–20 (HN 4370–89) were given 60 h.p. B.T.H. motors. The last of these actually entered service in 1926, the year before Chesterfield Corporation tried out some of this breed (e.g. RA 1823). Thereafter, Straker-Cloughs ceased to find British customers, who began to turn towards Guy, English Electric, Karriers and A.E.C. for their trackless trolleys.

## Sunbeam MS2. Pl. 153

In 1931 Sunbeam decided that with so much tram replacement going on in England there might be room for another competitor in the trolleybus manu-facturing field. Whereas, trading under the initials S.M.C., Sunbeam had hardly been a success in the motorbus sphere, they almost immediately found fame and favour under two wires. Perhaps because of their comparative lack of prowess in the bus world, they tried to make a distinctively electric vehicle, rather than alter an existing motorbus to electric instead of internal combustion operation, as had happened, for example, in the case of A.E.C. with their 661 and 661T chassis.

The MS2 was their first endeavour and some of the first went to Wolver-hampton Corporation as their Nos. 512–4 (JW 992–4) which had 59-seat Weymann bodies. The MS2 had three axles and was 30 ft. long. In 1933 one was sent to Bournemouth for testing against two A.E.Cs and a Thornycroft. It won the day and No. 68 (LJ 7701) was followed by 102 more MS2s over the period 1934–6. Apart from Nos. 78–83 (AEL 406–11), which possessed English Electric bodies, the remainder, (Nos, 72–7, AEL 400–5; 84–9, ALJ 60–5; 90–125, ALJ 964–99; 126–49, BEL 811–34 and 150–73, BRU 1–24), all had Park Royal bodywork. All these MS2 trolleybuses had dual entrances exits, two staircases and 59 seats. All were powered by 80 h.p. B.T.H. 101 motors. Because of the steep gradient of Richmond Hill leading out of Bournemouth Square, at the end of 1934, run back brakes were fitted to all these vehicles. Walsall Corporation, which ran joint trolleybus working with its neighbour, Wolverhampton, purchased MS2s in 1933 with a variety of bodies, Beadle (Nos. 155–9, ADH 1–5), Short Bros. (Nos. 160–4, ADH 6–10) and Weymanns (Nos. 165–9, ADH 11–15). Park Royal bodied MS2s came later in 1938 (Nos. 187/8, BDH 863/4) and 1940 (Nos. 216–19, HDH 211–14). Birmingham Corporation bought a solitary MS2 in 1934 (No. 67, OC 6567) with a M.C.W. 59-seat body.

Portsmouth tried out a modified version, the MS3, in 1934. No. 14 (RV 4662) had a 60-seat M.C.W. body and B.T.H. motors. Wolverhampton, needless to say, also took delivery of some of these less common Sunbeams (Nos. 96–8, 204/5 and 214–17), also in 1934.

## Sunbeam MF2

The prototype four wheel chassis for a 27 ft. long body, produced by Sunbeams and called the MF1, appeared in 1934, when four went to Wolverhampton Corporation as Nos. 206–9 (JW 4106–9) bearing 32 seat rear entrance Park Royal bodywork.

The MF2 was designed, however, for double-deck operation. Portsmouth Corporation tried out two MF2s in 1934; No. 8 (RV 4656) had a 50 seat English Electric body and No. 10 (RV 4660) had a similar M.C.W. body. Both had B.T.H. motors. Two years later Reading Corporation also tried out a brace of MF2s; both No. 1 (RD 8085) and No. 6 (RD 8090) had Park Royal lowbridge bodies and B.T.H. motors.

Wolverhampton Corporation bought thirty-eight MF2s in small batches between 1936 and 1942. These had double-deck bodies by Beadles, Roe and Park Royal, seating either 54 or 55 passengers. In 1936, however, there was an additional consignment of three single-deckers with Park Royal 32-seat rear entrance bodies (Nos. 231–3, JW 8131–3).

## Sunbeam/Karrier W4. Pl. 154, 155

Just as Guy Motors were one of the very few manufacturers allowed to build motorbuses during the latter half of the Second World War, so Sunbeam and their subsidiary Karrier (acquired in 1935) were the sole constructors of trolleybuses during those dark times. The Wartime 4 was made on utility lines, a counterpart to the Guy Arab Marks I &

II. Normally, it was expected that a 26 ft. long angular double-deck body would be fitted to the chassis.

The first Sunbeam W4s appeared in 1942 in the shape of Bradford Corporation Nos. 693–9 (DKW 993–9) and 700–2 (DKY 2–4) with Weymann 56-seat bodies. By 1943 production had really got under way. Maidstone Corporation received Nos. 54/5 (GKN 379/80) with Park Royal bodies and B.T.H. 207A–1 motors. Reading had similar trolleybuses with their Nos. 132–7 (BRD 797–801/14), as did Walsall with their Nos. 225/6 (JDH 29/30). Weymann bodwork being supplied for Wolverhampton's Nos. 296–9/400/1 (DJW 596–601), as was the case with Nottingham Corporation's Nos. 442–5 (GTV 42–5), the latter bearing Karrier manufacturing plates. Doncaster Corporation's Nos. 69–71 (CDT 312–4) were Karriers with Park Royal bodywork.

By 1944 production of the W4 had got really under way. In that fateful year Karrier plated W4s appeared at Ipswich (Nos. 87–90, PV 6875–8), Llanelly (CBX 530–3) and Nottingham (nos. 452–8, GTV 652–8); ones with Sunbeam names came to Maidstone (Nos. 56–8, GKP 511–3), Tees-side (Nos. 10–3, CPY 308–11 & 15–8, CPY 286–9), Derby (Nos. 171/2, RC 8471/2) and Wolverhampton (Nos. 402–7, DJW 902–7). South Lancs had two batches of Sunbeam W4s during 1944, Nos. 60–3 (FTD 452–5) with G.E.C. 80 h.p. motors and Nos. 64/5 (FTE 152/3) with English Electric 80 h.p. motors. Darlington Corporation at this juncture received thirteen single deckers with Brush 33-seat central entrance bodies and Metro-Vick motors (GHN 561–76), similar to those taken into stock the previous year (GHN 401–8).

Among new owners of the Karrier W4 in 1945 was St. Helens Corporation with Nos. 105–14 (DJ 9183–92) with Roe 50 seat lowbridge bodies. Sunbeam W4s found their way into the fleets of Kingston-upon-Hull (Nos. 67–78, GRH 287–98 and Pontypridd (FTG 234/5).

## Thornycroft J

In 1919 Thornycrofts started building J type chassis for double-deckers. These chassis stood high off the ground, like the old A.E.C. B and some of them possessed bodies with as many as seven slats in their guard rails beneath the sides of the bodywork. Portsmouth bought ten of these Js and had Wadham 34-seat open top bodies fitted to Nos. 1–10 (BK 2978/7/9–86). A 4 cylinder 30 h.p. engine was the power unit and the transmission was through a 4 speed gearbox with a gate change. Glasgow Corporation purchased a pair of Js and had 30 seat dual entrance/exit single-deck bus bodies constructed in 1924 for Nos. 13/4 (GB 6912/3). Southdown Motor Services had Harrington charabanc bodies fitted to No. 30 (CD 6353 : 32-seats) and No. 31 (CD 5379 : 27-seats); another charabanc example was to be found in Dundee Corporation's TS 3229/30.

At the 1923 Commercial Motor Show Thornycrofts displayed a 50-seat open top J with a more powerful, 50 h.p. engine, in the livery of the Cambrian Company. Among the last Js to be assembled seem to have been four with 32-seat rear entrance bus bodies for Aberdeen Corporation (Nos. 16–19, RS 7003–6) in 1925.

The J was a 4½ ton chassis model, and the same engine was used for the Thornycroft X, which weighed only three tons. This had a wheelbase of 15 ft. 6 ins.

## Thornycroft Boadicea

During the mid-'twenties Thornycrofts produced their BC model, sometimes referred to as the Boadicea, as in the case of the Cowieson bodied 29-seat dual entrance/exit buses run by Kilmarnock Corporation, (SD 8811–3/35–9), of 1924 vintage. It had a 33·8 h.p. 6 cylinder engine with a bore of 95 mm and a stroke of 127 mm. The BC, so it was claimed at the 1927 Show, was capable of travelling at up to 60 m.p.h. on the flat and averaged 10 m.p.h. in first gear when climbing the notorious Lynmouth Hill, with its 1 in 4¼ gradient.

The BC came in two forms, both of which had a wheelbase of 16 ft. 6 ins. As the normal control version, it found favour with Perth Corporation during 1926, (Nos. 10–12, GS 141/2 and 179), with their 26-seat rear entrance Croall bodies. However, in its forward control styling, it could carry more, e.g. Perth's No. 5 (GS 616) had room for 32 seated passengers, as did Nos. 36–47 (LJ 1600–11) owned by Bournemouth Corporation and which had assorted bodies by Martins, Strachans and Beadle.

The 4 cylinder version of the BC was called the UB. This had a 4¾ in./6 in. bore/stroke relationship, but had the same chassis and wheelbase as the BC. The normal control UB sat 28 to 30 passengers as against 30 to 32 of the UBF forward control model. Kilmarnock bought five of these latter with Northern Counties 28-seat dual entrance/exit bodywork (AG 2278/9 and 3194–6).

A slightly less powerful member of this family was the SB with a bore of 4⅜ in and a stroke of 5½ in. It sat between 24 and 26 passengers.

## Thornycroft A1

An advertisement appearing in the *Commercial Motor* in 1925 shows XY 2101, a new Thornycroft A1 belonging to the Great Western Railway Company. Furthermore, we are offered the information that recent War Office trials had shown that the A1 qualified for their subsidy since it was able to (1) climb hills of a gradient of 1 in 4½ carrying a full load, (2) traverse water 18 inches deep, (3) pull itself through ten inches of soft sand and finally, (4) travel at speeds of up to 40 m.p.h. at a rate of 17 m.p.g.

The A1 had a wheelbase of 11 ft. 6 in. and a 22·5 h.p. 4 cylinder engine with bore/stroke dimensions of 3¾ in./5 in. It was designed to seat between fourteen to eighteen passengers. Aberdeen Corporation had a 14-seater charabanc version (No. 58, RS 9702) in 1929, along with two others in this format, but seating 18 (Nos. 56/7, RS 9700/1). Venture of Bassingstoke, (the A1's home town,) had two in 1926 with 20 seat Vickers front entrance bus bodywork (Nos. 1/2, OT 1037/8), and followed them up with a third in 1927; No. 7 (OT 6768) had a 20-seat Wadhams body.

By extending the wheelbase to 14 ft. the A1 Long could seat more passengers. Hence Aberdeen's Nos. 27–34 (RS 7407–14) had a capacity for 23 and their No. 36 (RS 7284) for 25.

Great Southern Railway of Ireland bought a dozen of the A1s successor, A2, in 1930. Nos. 600–11 had either 20- or 19-seat bus bodies. A thirteenth vehicle in this batch (No. 612, Z1 5201) was of the A2 Long variety, but still sat 20, presumably with more leg room. Perth Corporation invested in several of this latter type, Nos. 16–21 had 20-seat Croall bodywork.

## Tilling-Stevens Petrol-Electric TS Series. Pl. 46

'Just pull the field lever slightly towards you, the engine retains its speed and you progress uphill with the same smoothness as on the level, unhaunted by the fear that the engine will "lay-down" when you're half-way up.' So runs an advertisement in the *Commerical Motor* of 1919 for the petrol-electric TS3 model, which was selling so well to Southdown and other operators. The TS3 had no gears.

Like so many chassis of this vintage the TS3 could take almost any kind of bodywork, for it stood well clear of the ground. Southdown had it for 32-seater charabancs (e.g. Nos. 81/2, CD 1581/5642), for 30-seater buses (e.g. No. 83, CD 1583) and for 51-seat open top double-deckers

(e.g. 91–6, CD 6891–6). Also among earlier customers was Walsall Corporation who, in 1919, took delivery of DH 1456/7, TS3s with Dodson 28-seat rear entrance bus bodies. Similar vehicles followed in 1920 (DH 1204 and 1903–5). Nearby West Bromwich Corporation tried out a TS3 with a Roberts 29-seat front entrance body (No. 5, EA 999) in 1920, followed by a second vehicle (No. 4, EA 302) with a 25-seat W. J. Smith body in 1921. Potteries Electric Traction had four with 29-seat bodies in 1920 (Nos. 17–20, EH 1860/1/8/9).

At the Fifth Commercial Motor Show (1921) Tilling-Stevens brought out two more petrol-electric models. The TS4 was a four tonner with a 4 cylinder engine of bore/stroke dimensions of 4¾ in./6 in. and a wheelbase of 14 ft. 6 ins., overall length being 24 ft. 6 ins. This could cope with a double-deck body seating 57. The other was the TS5, a two tonner planned as a 20 seater. It had a 4 cylinder engine with bore/stroke of 105 mm/125 mm, a wheelbase of 12 ft. and an overall length of 18 ft. 10 ins.

In 1923 came the TS6, which had a 50 h.p. engine, a wheelbase of 15 ft. 3 ins. and was normally used for single-deck buses, although Southdown in 1925 did have eleven which received 51 seat Tilling double-deck open top bodywork (Nos. 226–36, CD 9226–36). More typical seems to have been Leicester Corporation's Nos. 1–8 (BC 9162–9) with their Brush 32-seat rear entrance bodies followed by Nos. 9–14 (RY 1574–9) in 1925. Wolverhampton not only bought seventeen TS6 buses fitted with Dodson or Fleming bodies seating anything from 32 to 38 passengers (Nos. 24–35/40/1/4–6), but also some of the rare TS6 trolley-buses (Nos. 1–32) with Dodson 36- or 40-seat central entrance bodies. Ipswich Corporation also tried out a TS6 trolleybus in 1925; No. 5 (DX 5217) had a locally built 30-seat front entrance Ransomes body.

Another rare form of the TS was the Dennis-Stevens petrol electric, of which fourteen found their way into the fleet of Walsall Corporation; DH 1452–5 (1919); DH 1900–2 (1920) and DH 2180–6 (1920). All had 28-seat rear entrance Dodson bodywork.

A six-wheeled version of the petrol-electric, the TS15, went into the fleet of Wolverhampton Corporation in 1928; No. 66 (UK 5366) had a 66-seat Dodson body, complete with roof and enclosed staircase. This vehicle had a 95 b.h.p. engine, whereby the drive was taken to the bogie axles by a cardon shaft. The final drive was by underneath worms. All the wheels ran on taper-roller bearings.

### Tilling-Stevens Express. Pl. 47, 48

A more orthodox form of the TS series was wanted by some clients of Tilling-Stevens, and so at the 1925 Commercial Motor Show they were able to examine the Express with its 40 h.p. 4 cylinder engine, designed for a 32-seater bus. By the time the Eighth Show arrived two years later this model had diversified into several sub-forms as set out below.

| Model | Seats | Wheelbase |
|-------|-------|-----------|
| B9A | 32 | 15 ft. 6 ins. |
| B9B | 30 | 15 ft. 6 ins. |
| B10A | 32 | 15 ft. 6 ins. |
| B10B | 30 | 15 ft. 6 ins. |
| B10C | 40 | 17 ft. 0 ins. |

All were powered by a 4 cylinder engine with a bore of $4\frac{1}{4}$ in. and a stroke of $5\frac{1}{2}$ in.

Examples of the B9A can be found in Marlow & District's Nos. 4/5 (MO 9316/27) with their 35-seat rear entrance Brush bodies of 1927, which had formerly been part of a batch of fourteen in the fleet of neighbouring Thames Valley (Nos. 144–57). Southdown were interested in the B9B for their 1926–7 vintage coaches with 30-seat rear entrance bodies by Harringtons (Nos. 401–30/8), Tillings (Nos. 431–7) and London Lorries (Nos. 439–44).

The B10 Series with that operator served a variety of purposes. B10B2s Nos. 480–3 (UF 3080–3) received 20-seat Harrington luxury coach bodywork for use on extended tours of Devon, and B10A2s Nos. 484–94 (UF 3584, etc.) had either Harrington or Tillings 32-seat bus bodies. One vehicle is of particular interest; B10A2 No. 460 (UF 4300) was given an all-metal 48-seat open top double-deck body by Shorts. Another large operator to enjoy using the Express was North Western Road Car. They followed up their TS series with several batches of the B10A2 version (DB 5291–9, 9300–15/7–97, 9416–77). Portsmouth Corporation sampled the B10A2 for a pair of 30-seat buses with Park Royal bodywork (Nos. 1/2, RV 236/7).

A lightweight version, the 6 cylinder B39, was employed by Southdown to overcome the weight restrictions on the bridge linking Hayling Island to the mainland. Nos. 1216–21 (ACD 716–21) with their Short Bros. 26-seat bodies were to be found in the years following 1933 on route 47. They were of the B39A6 variety. Eastern National had 32-seat Beadle bodywork fitted to their B39A7s in 1932 (Nos. 3309–16). Another version, the 4 cylinder B49A7 was to be found in the fleet of West Yorkshire (Nos. 713–42, WX 8972–9001), with their Lowestoft-constructed Eastern Counties 34-seat front entrance bodies. A 36-seat B49A7 went to Happy Days of Stafford in 1932 (No. 12, VT 7591).

### Tilling-Stevens 60 Model

A 6 cylinder petrol engine with a bore of 102 mm appeared in 1932 as the C6OA7, called the Express Six. Southdown bought three and Nos. 200–2 (UF 8030–2) received 31-seat rear entrance bus bodies built by Harringtons of Hove. In 1934 this model was replaced by the D6OA7, of which BKE 653 with its Duple 32-seat coach body is an example. However, contemporary with these two versions of the Express Six was the E6OA6, which was to be found in the ranks of Portsmouth Corporation; Nos. 75–84 (RV 1135–9/41–7) had 50-seat English Electric bodies, in common with most Pompey double-decked vehicles of this era. Walsall also purchased an E6OA6; No. 101 (DH 9043) was given a 53-seat Beadle body.

If this model had a Gardner 5LW oil engine as an option it became a D5LA6, while the 6 cylinder Gardner converted it into a D6LA6 model.

## Vulcan VSD. Pl. 49, 50

At the 1921 Olympia Vulcan displayed a 20-seater coach and a 22-seater bus. These were probably of the VSD type with its small wheels, which made it suitable for seaside duties. With this in mind, Skegness Motor Services began to buy one or two each season and have 25-seat toastrack bodywork fitted by Eatons. Thus in 1924 there arrived at the famous Clock Tower NR 4223, followed by NR 6648 (1925), NR 7266 (1925), FU 5946 (1926) and FU 7549 (1927). In 1934 these passed into the hands of the Lincolnshire Road Car Company, who found plenty of seasonable service still surviving in them. Over in the Isle of Man, Douglas Corporation ran a VSD that carried as many as forty seated passengers (MAN 124). Southdown had four with 14-seat Harrington charabanc bodies (Nos. 301–4, CD 7101–4), and later acquired an 18-seater chara. from Tricksey of West Wittering (BP 7485) as their No. 305 and two from Dowle of Singleton (BP 7489 and BP 8429) as their Nos. 309/10.

At the 1927 Commercial Motor Show the VSD seems to have been succeeded by the 3XB with its four cylinder Vulcan engine (bore 85 mm; stroke 130 mm) and wheelbase of 11 ft. 10¼ ins.

## Vulcan Prince

Other 1927 models included a 6 cylinder version of the 3XB, the 3XS with a wheelbase of 12 ft. 5½ ins. and a bore/stroke of 69 mm/120 mm. However, two larger single-decker chassis were introduced at this stage. The VWB had a 4 cylinder engine of 110 mm/140 mm dimensions and a wheelbase of 15 ft. 4 ins., designed to seat 30 passengers. The VWBL only differed by having a wheelbase two *inches* longer! By 1931 this chassis was being called the Prince. Happy Days of Stafford took two of these fitted with 32-seat bus bodies (No. 7, VT 6025 and No. 9, RF 8189).

A double-decker version, called the Emperor attracted Glasgow Corporation in 1931. They ordered twenty-five of these and asked Cowiesons to build 48-seat bodies for Nos. 350–74 (GG 2126–53).

## W & G Two Tonner. Pl. 51

In 1919 W & G Du Cros introduced their two ton chassis which had a whcelbase of 11 ft. 3 ins. and an overall chassis length of 17 ft. 6 ins. This was powered by a Dorman 4 cylinder engine of the old L headed type, with a bore of 95 mm and a stroke of 140 mm, which developed 35 b.h.p. at 1,500 r.p.m. Transmission was through a cone clutch and a 4 speed gearbox.

By the 1923 Commercial Motor Show the wheelbase had been lengthened to 13 ft., which meant an increase in the seating available. A 4 cylinder monoblock type of engine was fitted.

The 1925 Olympia Show had on display a successor to the Two Tonner. This was a 6 cylinder model with an R.C.A. rating of 33·5 h.p., with bore/stroke dimensions of 95·2 mm/126·9 mm, and developing 70 b.h.p. at 2,200 r.p.m. The wheelbase of this new model was 15 ft. 8½ ins., giving an overall chassis length of 22 ft. 5 ins. and a width of 6 ft. 10 ins. In 1927 this was called the Talbot Senior. As such it found favour with Bournemouth Corporation, who ordered three of these vehicles for their 1927 season. Nos. 16–8 (RU 5833–5) had Du Cros 25-seat front entrance bodywork too. They were followed next year by two more similar batches, this time bearing Strachan & Brown bodies (Nos. 19–21, RU 7327–9 and 22–7, RU 8021–6). Finally in 1929 came a trio (Nos. 28–30, RU 9505–7) with Hall Lewis bodywork.

The 1927 Commercial Motor Show saw the debut of the W25 Talbot Junior. This had only a 4 cylinder engine (bore 101·5 mm, stroke 140 mm) and was designed to seat 20 passengers. Bream of Hemel Hempstead, Hertfordshire, bought one (TM 9017).

At the same time a scaled down 6 cylinder chassis, the MAB, was put onto the market with a wheelbase reduced to 11 ft. 9 ins. The bore/stroke of this unit were 3 in./4¾ in. Happy days of Stafford purchased one of these 14-seaters (RF 6032) in 1929.

## W & G Freighter

In 1929 Du Cros decided to compete with Shelvoke & Drewry over the market for a really low framed small bus. Like the other Freighter the W & G version had tiny wheels with solid tyres. The original model was powered by an engine that developed 31·5 b.h.p. at 1,500 r.p.m. The wheelbase was a mere 9 ft. 3½ ins.

Three years later a more powerful unit was brought out for the Freighter. This 20 h.p. engine with its bore of 90 mm and stroke of 130 mm developed 48 b.h.p. Transmission was via overhead worm to the rear axle. Neither version of the Freighter, in fact, found a market with the main seaside operators as had been hoped, who continued to support Shelvoke & Drewry and others in this field.

# SOME OTHER BRITISH MANUFACTURERS BETWEEN 1919 AND 1939

A.J.S.
AUSTIN
B.A.T.
BEAN
BEARDMORE
BURFORD
CALEDON
CHURCHILL
CLEMENT-TALBOT
CLYDE
CLYDESDALE

F.W.D. (= Four Wheel Drive)
GARNER
GRAHAM-DODGE
HALLEY
LANCHESTER
McCURD
MORRIS-COMMERCIAL
NAPIER
STRAKER-SQUIRE
SURREY-DODGE
WHITE

# SOME OTHER FOREIGN MANUFACTURED BUSES AND COACHES BOUGHT BY BRITISH OPERATORS BETWEEN 1919 AND 1939

BERLIET.   2 Tonner
           CT6
CITROEN.
DE DION.   JE2
DODGE.   KB, MC, PLB, RB, RBF,
         SBF
FAGEOL.
FEDERAL.   U, W
FIAT.
GARFORD.
G.M.C.   T19, T20, T30, T40, T42
GOTFRIEDSON.   2 Tonner

INTERNATIONAL.   15
LAFFLEY.   LC2
LATIL.   B2, 30 Cwt., LVL
MINERVA.
OPEL.
REPUBLIC.
RENAULT.
SEABROOK-NAPOLEON.
STUDEBAKER.
UNIC.   MIA 2
WALLACE.
WILLYS OVERLAND.

*A.E.C. Fifty Years,* (A.E.C. 1962).

*Barton Diamond Jubilee 1908–1968* (E. Midlands Area Omnibus Enthusiasts Soc. 1969).

*Birkenhead & District, Local Transport in,* T. B. Maund, (Omnibus Society 1965).

*Birmingham City Transport, Pt. I: 1903–1940,* (P.S.V. Circle & Omnibus Soc. 1968).

*Birmingham City Transport: Part I: Trams & Trolleybuses,* W. A. Camwell, (Ian Allan 1950).

*Birmingham City Transport: Part II: Buses,* W. A. Camwell, (Ian Allan 1950).

*Black & White Motorways Ltd.,* (P.S.V. Circle & Omnibus Soc. 1967).

*Blackburn Buses, 40 Years of, 1929–1969* (Blackburn Corp. 1969).

*Bournemouth Corporation Transport,* J. Mawson (Advertiser Press 1967).

*Bournemouth Trolleybuses: Official Souvenir Brochure 1933–1969,* by David L. Chalk, (Bournemouth Corporation 1969).

*Bradford Trolleybuses, 1911–1960,* Harold Brearley, (Oakwood Press 1960).

*Brighton Corporation Transport, 1901–1967,* (Worthing Historic Vehicle Group 1967).

*Brighton & Hove, The Trolleybuses of,* David Kaye & Martin Nimmo, (Reading Transport Soc. 1968).

*Bristol Tramways Vehicles, A.B.C. of,* (Ian Allan 1949).

*Bristol Omnibus Company Ltd., Part II: 1937–1960,* (P.S.V. Circle & Omnibus Soc. 1968).

*British Bus Services, The History of,* John Hibbs, (David & Charles 1968).

*British Double-Deckers Since 1942,* A. A. Townsin, (Modern Transport Publishing Co. 1965).

*Bus Stop,* an anthology compiled by Gavin Booth, (Ian Allan 1969).

*Buses, Trolleys & Trams,* Chas. S. Dunbar, (Paul Hamlyn 1967).

*Cardiff, 67 years of Electric Transport in,* (National Trolleybus Assoc. 1970).

*Cheltenham's Trams and Buses, 1890–1963,* J. P. Appleby & F. Lloyd, (21 Tram Group 1964).

*City of Oxford,* (Omnibus Soc. 1966).

*City of Oxford Motor Services Ltd.,* (P.S.V. Circle & Omnibus Soc. 1969).

*Colchester Corporation 1904–1954,* (Colchester Corporation).

*Coras Iompair Eireann,* Gerard Brazil, (P.S.V. Circle, Omnibus Soc. & Tramway Museum Soc. of Ireland 1965).

*Devon General, A History of,* (P.S.V. Circle, Omnibus Soc. & Ian Allan 1966).

*Doncaster Corporation Transport,* (P.S.V. Circle & Omnibus Soc. 1964).

*Don Everall Ltd.,* (P.S.V. Circle & Omnibus Soc. 1962).

*Dublin's Buses,* P. J. Flanagan & C. B. Mac and tSaoir, (Transport Research Associates 1968).

*Eastbourne Corporation Transport Department 1903–1963,* (Eastbourne Corporation).

*East Kent Buses and Coaches,* S. L. Poole, (Ian Allan 1949).

*Eastern Municipalities, Motorbuses, Trolleybuses and Trams of* (P.S.V. Circle & Omnibus Soc. 1969).

*Eastern National Omnibus Company, Part I: 1930–1954,* (P.S.V. Circle & Omnibus Soc. 1965).

*East Lindsey, Lincs., P.S.V. Operators of,* P. R. White & A. Tye, (Lincs. Transport Review 1966).

*Edinburgh's Transport,* D. L. G. Hunter, (Advertiser Press 1964).

*Essex & Suffolk, The Small Stage Carriage Operators of,* (P.S.V. Circle & Omnibus Soc. 1967).

*Feathers in their Cap (Story of Guy Motors),* Robin N. Hannay, (Omnibus Soc. 1960).

*First Thirty Years (Story of the London Bus, 1904–1933),* (Dryhurst 1962).

*Freighters on the Front (Story of Shelvoke & Drewry Buses),* David Kaye, (Kaye 1963 with P.S.V. Circle Supplement 1968).

*Glasgow Corporation,* (Ian Allan British Bus Fleets No. 20).

*Gosport & Fareham Omnibus Company Ltd.,* (P.S.V. Circle & Omnibus Soc. 1964).

*Grey-Green Story, The,* T. McLachlan, (Omnibus Soc. 1962).

*Hants & Dorset Motor Services Ltd.: Pt. 1: 1916 to 1938,* (P.S.V. Circle & Omnibus Soc. 1968).

*Hants & Dorset Motor Services Ltd.: Pt. 2: 1939 to 1968,* (P.S.V. Circle & Omnibus Soc. 1969).

*Herefordshire, Warwickshire & Worcestershire, The Small Stage Carriage Operators of* (P.S.V. Circle & Omnibus Soc. 1966).

*Holland, Lincs., The Bus Operators of,* David Kaye, (Lincs. Transport Review 1966).

*Huddersfield Trolleybus System, The,* (West Riding Trolleybus Soc. 1968).

*Huddersfield Trolleybus System,* (Huddersfield Trolleybus Preservation Soc. 1968).

*Ireland, The Small Stage Carriage Operators of,* Gerard Brazil, (P.S.V. Circle, Omnibus Soc. & Tramway Museum Soc. of Ireland 1966).

*Jersey, Transport in,* Michael Ginns, (Transport World 1961).

*Keighley Corporation Transport,* J. S. King, (Advertiser Press 1964).

*Kingsland Road (Story of a London road),* A. W. McCall, (Omnibus Soc. 1958).

*Ledgard Fleet, The,* M. H. Lockyer, (R. Wickens 1962).

*Leicester City Transport, Vehicles owned Past and Present 1924–1968* (East Midlands Area Omnibus Enthusiasts Soc. 1969).

*Lincolnshire Wolds, P.S.V. Operators of the,* P. R. White & A. Tye, (Lincs. Transport Review 1966).

*Londonderry & Lough Swilly Railway,* C. J. D. Orchard, (P.S.V. Circle, Omnibus Soc. & Tramway Museum Soc. of Ireland 1966).

*London Bus & Tram Album,* (1st Ed. Ian Allan 1963; 2nd Ed. 1968).

*London Trams and Trolleybuses in 1948,* (Ian Allan 1968).

*London Motor-Bus 1896–1968, The,* R. W. Kidner, (Oakwood Press 1968).

*London Transport Buses & Coaches,* E. J. Smith, (Ian Allan 1950).

*London Country Bus, The,* J. S. Wagstaff, (Oakwood Press 1968).

*London General, 1856–1956,* (London Transport).

*London Transport Bus Services in the St. Albans Area 1933–1959,* A. W. McCall, (Omnibus Soc. 1960).

*London Transport and Its Predecessors, The Vehicles of, series,* (P.S.V. Circle & Omnibus Soc.):—

    *The 'Q' Class,* (1961).

    *The Bristol 'B' Class and other Bristol Vehicles,* (1962).

    *The 'GF' Class and other Gilford Vehicles,* (1963).

*London Trolleybuses,* (Dryhurst 1962).

*London's Trolleybuses* (P.S.V. Circle & Omnibus Soc. 1969).
*Luton Corporation Transport*, (P.S.V. Circle & Omnibus Soc. 1962).
*Maidstone & District Buses & Coaches*, (Ian Allan 1950).
*Metropolitan Traffic Area, The Small Stage Carriage Operators of*, (P.S.V. Circle & Omnibus Soc. 1966).
*Midland Red Buses & Coaches*, (Ian Allan 1948).
*Midland Red, Part I: 1904–1933*, (P.S.V. Circle & Omnibus Soc. 1961).
*Midland Red, Part II: 1933–1959*, (P.S.V. Circle & Omnibus Soc. 1959).
*Newport Corporation Omnibus List*, (Monmouthshire Railway Soc. 1961).
*Norfolk, The Small Stage Carriage Operators of*, (P.S.V. Circle & Omnibus Soc. 1960).
*Nottingham's Trolleybus System*, C. F. Riley, (Omnibus Soc. 1966).
*Overground (Story of London's Transport 1900–1947)*, (Ian Allan 1947).
*Portsmouth, City of, Passenger Transport Department 1901–1964*, (Worthing Historic Vehicle Group 1964).
*Portsmouth, The Trolleybuses of*, D. A. P. Janes and R. G. Funnell, (Reading Transport Soc. 1969).
*Potteries Motor Traction Company Ltd.*, (P.S.V. Circle & Omnibus Soc. 1968).
*Premier (Story of a London Pirate)*, (Dryhurst 1962).
*Premier Travel Ltd.*, Cambridge, (P.S.V. Circle & Omnibus Soc. 1966).
*Provincial Bus & Tram Album*, J. Joyce, (Ian Allan 1968).
*Reading Corporation Transport*, (P.S.V. Circle & Omnibus Soc. 1961).
*Rhondda Transport Company Ltd.*, (P.S.V. Circle & Omnibus Soc. 1967).
*St. Helens, The Trolleybuses of*, Geoffrey Sandford, (Reading Transport Soc. 1968).
*Scottish Municipalities, The Motorbuses & Trolleybuses of the*, (P.S.V. Circle & Omnibus Soc. 1962).
*Seventy-five Years on Wheels (Barrow-in-Furness 1895–1960)*, Ian L. Cormack, (Scottish Tramway Museum Soc. 1960).
*Shropshire, The Small Stage Carriage Operators of*, (P.S.V. Circle & Omnibus Soc. 1963).
*Silent Service (Story of Bournemouth Trolleybuses)*, David L. Chalk, (P.S.V. Circle & Omnibus Soc. 1962).
*Southdown Buses & Coaches*, (Ian Allan 1950).
*Southdown Motor Services Ltd.*, (P.S.V. Circle & Omnibus Soc. 1957).
*Southdown Story, The, 1915–1965*, (Southdown Motor Services).
*South Eastern Municipalities, Motor Buses, Trolleybuses and Trams of the*, (P.S.V.Circle & Omnibus Soc. 1969).
*Staffordshire, The Small Stage Carriage Operators of*, (P.S.V. Circle & Omnibus Soc. 1965).
*Teesside Trolleybuses, 50 years of, 1919–1969*, (National Trolleybus Assoc. 1969).
*Thames Valley Traction Company Ltd.*, (P.S.V. Circle & Omnibus Soc. 1960).
*Trolleybus Trails*, J. Joyce, (Ian Allan 1963).
*Veteran & Vintage Public Service Vehicles*, David Kaye, (Ian Allan 1962).
*West Midlands Municipalities, The Trams, Motor Buses & Trolleybuses of*, (P.S.V. Circle & Omnibus Soc. 1965).
*Western Municipalities, Motor Buses and Trams of*, (P.S.V. Circle & Omnibus Soc. 1963).
*Wheels of Service (Story of P.M.T. 1898–1958)*, (Potteries).
*Wilts & Dorset Motor Services Ltd.*, (P.S.V. Circle & Omnibus Soc. 1963).
*Yorkshire Traffic Area, The Small Stage Carriage Operators of, Part I*, (P.S.V. Circle & Omnibus Soc. 1967).

In addition:

*Buses Illustrated*, (called *Buses* as from April 1968), No. 1 (Nov. 1949) onwards.
*Commercial Motor*, (since 1905).
*Con-rod*, (organ of Lincolnshire Vintage Vehicle Society, since 1961).
*Old Motor*, (since 1963).
*Transport History*, (since March 1968).
*Trolleybus*, (organ of Reading Transport Society, since January 1967).
*Vintage Commercial*, (since 1962–3).

# SOME PRESERVED BUSES AND TROLLEYBUSES OF THE PERIOD
## 1919–1945

Many of these in the list following have been restored to their former glory and others are still in quite a dilapidated state, but there is an intention to restore them when time and money become available. Some, however, like Southdown No. 228 (FUF 228), a Leyland Titan TD5, were preserved, but due to lack of finance had to be scrapped after all. Some are owned by individuals, some by societies, some by museums. All listed below are, at the time of compilation, resident within the confines of Great Britain.

The usual system of symbols has been employed in describing the vehicles that follow, viz.:

Bus codes: before seating capacity—

    B   = Single-decker bus

    C   = Single-decker coach

    Ch  = Charabanc

    DP = Single-decker dual purpose vehicle

    H   = Highbridge type of double-decker

    L   = Lowbridge type of double-decker (i.e. sunken gangway on upper deck)

    O   = Open-top double-decker

    T   = Toastrack type of single-decker

Body codes: after seating capacity—

    C   = Central entrance

    D   = Dual entrance/exit

    F   = Front entrance

    R   = Rear entrance

    ROS = Rear entrance with open staircase

             BT = Breakdown Tender      TW = Tower Wagon

Question marks or blank spaces indicate that the information is not available. All the bodies named in the following list were those on the chassis at the time of compilation.

| Chassis Type | Date | Body Details | Reg. No. | Original Owner |
|---|---|---|---|---|
| A.D.C. 423 | 1927 | B—R | | East Yorkshire |
| A.E.C. K | 1920 | L.G.O.C. O46R | XC 8059 | L.G.O.C. K424 |
| A.E.C. S | 1922 | L.G.O.C. O54R | XL 8962 | L.G.O.C. S454 |
| A.E.C. S | 1923 | L.G.O.C. O54R | XM 7399 | L.G.O.C. S742 |
| A.E.C. NS | 1927 | L.G.O.C. H52R | YR 3844 | L.G.O.C. NS1955 |
| A.E.C. Regent | 1931 | United H48R | EX 2877 | Great Yarmouth 30 |
| A.E.C. Regent | 1931 | L.G.O.C. H48R | GK 3192 | L.G.O.C. ST821 |
| A.E.C. Regent | 1931 | Tillings H48R | GJ 2098 | L.G.O.C. ST922 |
| A.E.C. Regent | 1932 | Brush O52R | JO 5403 | City of Oxford GA16 |
| A.E.C. Regent | 1932 | Brighton, Hove & Dist. BT | GW 6274 | Tilling 6274 |
| A.E.C. Regent | 1933 | Brush H56R | OD 7489 | Devon General 202 |

| Chassis Type | Date | Body Details | Reg. No. | Original Owner |
|---|---|---|---|---|
| A.E.C. Regent | 1933 | Short O55R | OD 7497 | Devon General 210 |
| A.E.C. Regent | 1933 | Brush H56R | OD 7500 | Devon General 213 |
| A.E.C. Regent | 1934 | L.P.T.B. BT | JJ 4376 | L.P.T.B. STL159 |
| A.E.C. Regent | 1934 | L.P.T.B. H56R | AYV 651 | L.P.T.B. STL 469 |
| A.E.C. Regent | 1935 | Park Royal L52R | RD 7127 | Reading 47 |
| A.E.C. Regent | 1937 | L.P.T.B. H56R | DLU 92 | L.P.T.B. STL2093 |
| A.E.C. Regent | 1937 | L.P.T.B. H56R | DLU 240 | L.P.T.B. STL1871 |
| A.E.C. Regent | 1938 | L.P.T.B. H56R | EGO 426 | L.P.T.B. STL2377 |
| A.E.C. Regent | 1939 | Weymann H54R | FUF 63 | Brighton 63 |
| A.E.C. Regent | 1939 | N.C.M.E. H57R | DMN 650 | Douglas 50 |
| A.E.C. Regent | 1939 | L.P.T.B. H56R | FXT 219 | L.P.T.B. RT44 |
| A.E.C. Regent | 1939 | L.P.T.B. H56R | FXT 257 | L.P.T.B. RT113 |
| A.E.C. Renown | 1931 | L.G.O.C. H56R | GK 5323 | L.G.O.C. LT165 |
| A.E.C. Renown | 1939 | N.C.M.E. H64R | CBC 321 | Leicester 329 |
| A.E.C. Regal I | 1929 | L.G.O.C. B28F | UU 6646 | L.G.O.C. T31 |
| A.E.C. Regal I | 1930 | Duple C30F | GK 5486 | Green Line T219 |
| A.E.C. Regal I | 1931 | Craven B30 | VO 5323 | Red Bus |
| A.E.C. Regal I | 1934 | Leyland B20R | FV 4548 | Ribble 25 |
| A.E.C. Regal I | 1935 | Alexander DP32F | WS 4482 | S.M.T. B134 |
| A.E.C. Regal o662 | 1940 | Weymann B35F | DOD 474 | Devon General SR474 |
| A.E.C. Q | 1935 | B.R.C.W.C. B37C | BXD 576 | L.P.T.B. Q55 |
| A.E.C. Q | 1936 | B.R.C.W.C. B37C | CGJ 174 | L.P.T.B. Q69 |
| A.E.C. Q | 1936 | B.R.C.W.C. B37C | CGJ 188 | L.P.T.B. Q83 |
| A.E.C. 663T | 1931 | Union Construction H56R | HX 2756 | L.U.T. 1 |
| A.E.C. 663T | 1939 | Weymann H56R | CPM 61 | B. H. & D. 6340 |
| A.E.C. 661T | 1934 | English Electric H50R | RV 4649 | Portsmouth 1 |
| A.E.C. 661T | 1937 | Park Royal H56R | FW 8990 | Cleethorpes 54 |
| A.E.C. 661T | 1939 | Park Royal H56R | ARD 676 | Reading 113 |
| A.E.C. 664T | 1936 | M.C.W. H70R | CUL 260 | L.P.T.B. 260 |
| A.E.C. 664T | 1939 | N.C.M.E. H70R | CKG 193 | Cardiff 203 |
| A.E.C. 664T | 1940 | Harkness H68R | FZ 7883 | Belfast 98 |
| A.E.C. /M.C.W. Chassisless | 1939 | M.C.W. H70R | FXH 521 | L.P.T.B. 1521 |
| ALBION PH24 | 1927 | | RA 3829 | Duke of Devonshire |
| ALBION PM 28 | 1928 | Roe TW | EE 8128 | Grimsby 32 |
| ALBION SPLB41 | 1932 | C14F | US 6798 | A Glasgow convent |
| ALBION Valkyrie PW65 | 1932 | Alexander B34F | WG 1448 | Alexander F55 |
| ALBION Valiant PV70 | 1935 | Harrington C—F | LJ 9501 | Charlie Cars, Bournemouth |
| ALBION Victor PHB49 | 1935 | Abbott C20F | AAA 756 | King Alfred, Winchester |
| AUSTIN 22 h.p. | 1925 | Caselley T10 | TT 5132 | |

| Chassis Type | Date | Body Details | Reg. No. | Original Owner |
|---|---|---|---|---|
| AUSTIN 22 h.p. | 1927 | Dowell T13 | UO 1477 | Sidmouth Motor Co. |
| AUSTIN 22 h.p. | 1927 | Tiverton B13F | UO 2331 | Sidmouth Motor Co. |
| AUSTIN 22 h.p. | 1928 | Dowell T13 | UO 7095 | Sidmouth Motor Co. |
| BEAN | 1928 | | UL 1271 | |
| BEDFORD WHB | 1931 | Duple C14F | TM 9547 | J. Woodham, Melchbourne |
| BEDFORD WLB | 1931 | Duple C20F | MV 8996 | Howard, West Byfleet |
| BEDFORD WLB | 1934 | Duple B20F | AAF 66 | F. Greenslade, Dulverton |
| BEDFORD WLB | 1935 | Duple C20R | CMG 30 | Garner, Ealing |
| BEDFORD WTB | 1937 | Duple C29F | DDV 55 | Southern National 489 |
| BEDFORD WTB | 1939 | Duple C26F | CDL 920 | |
| BEDFORD WTB | 1939 | Duple C29F | EAL 113 | Gash, Newark |
| BEDFORD WTB | 1939 | Burlingham B25F | FEL 216 | Bournemouth 13 |
| BEDFORD WTB | 1939 | Burlingham B25F | FEL 218 | Bournemouth 15 |
| BEDFORD OWB | 1944 | Duple B27F | CTP 200 | Portsmouth 170 |
| BRISTOL K5G | 1938 | Roe L55R | CWT 671 | West Yorkshire KDG26 |
| BRISTOL K5G | 1938 | Weymann L48R | FKL 611 | Maidstone & District 273 |
| BRISTOL K5G | 1939 | E.C.W. L55R | AJN 825 | Westcliff-on-Sea |
| BRISTOL K5G | 1939 | Weymann H54R | GKE 68 | Chatham & District 874 |
| BRISTOL K5G | 1939 | Willowbrook L53R | AJA 152 | North Western 432 |
| BRISTOL K5G | 1939 | E.C.W. O56R | CDL 899 | Southern Vectis 702 |
| BRISTOL K5G | 1940 | E.C.W. O56R | CAP 211 | B. H. & D. 6356 |
| BRISTOL K5G | 1940 | E.C.W. O56R | CAP 234 | B. H. & D. 6350 |
| BRISTOL K5G | 1940 | E.C.W. O56R | DDL 50 | Southern Vectis 703 |
| BRISTOL K5G | 1940 | E.C.W. O56R | GHT 124 | Bristol C3312 |
| BRISTOL K6A | 1944 | Park Royal H56R | FNY 933 | Pontypridd 40 |
| BRISTOL K6A | 1945 | H & D O59R | FRU 308 | Hants & Dorset TD 777 |
| BRISTOL H | 1933 | Beadle B—R | FJ 8967 | Western National 137 |
| BRISTOL JJW6A | 1934 | Beadle B—R | ATT 922 | Western National 172 |
| BRISTOL JO5G | 1937 | E.C.W. B32F | BWT 794 | West Yorkshire |
| BRISTOL L5G | 1938 | Beadle BT | BOW 168 | Hants & Dorset TS 674 |
| BRISTOL L5G | 1939 | Burlingham B35R | AJA 118 | North Western 364 |
| BRISTOL L5G | 1941 | E.C.W. B35F | FHN 833 | Utd. Automobile BG 147 |
| CHEVROLET LQ | 1929 | Bush & Twiddy C14F | VF 6618 | |
| CHEVROLET LQ | 1931 | Bush & Twiddy C14F | VF 8157 | |
| COMMER PNF4 | 1936 | Roberts (Hastings) C26F | JG 7763 | |
| COMMER PN3 | 1937 | Waveney B20F | JC 4557 | Llandudno |
| DAIMLER COG5 | 1937 | M.C.W. H54R | CVP 207 | Birmingham 1107 |
| DAIMLER COG5-40 | 1939 | Willowbrook C39F | GNU 750 | Tailby & George (Willington) Dr. 5 |
| DAIMLER CWA6 | 1945 | Duple L55R | CCX 777 | Huddersfield 217 |
| DENNIS E | 1929 | Dixon B32F | EA 4181 | West Bromwich 32 |
| DENNIS GL | 1929 | Roberts T19 | CC 8694 | Llandudno |
| DENNIS GL | 1929 | Roberts T19 | CC 9305 | Llandudno |

| Chassis Type | Date | Body Details | Reg. No. | Original Owner |
|---|---|---|---|---|
| DENNIS GL | 1929 | Roberts T19 | CC 9424 | Llandudno |
| DENNIS 30 cwt. | 1929 | Short B18F | | |
| DENNIS Ace | 1934 | | AUB 354 | |
| DENNIS Ace | 1934 | East Kent B20F | JG 4234 | East Kent |
| DENNIS Ace | 1936 | Dennis C20C | CTW 210 | Eastern National 3614 |
| DENNIS Ace | 1938 | Mumford C20F | ECV 412 | Pearce, Polperro |
| DENNIS Mace | 1936 | | CYF 163 | |
| DENNIS Lancet I | 1936 | Park Royal B34 | JG 6809 | East Kent |
| DENNIS Falcon | 1939 | Dennis B30F | FUF 181 | Southdown 81 |
| DODGE | 1931 | Robson B14F | VK 5401 | Baty, Rookhope |
| FORD T | 1921 | Ruston & Hornsby B14 | EP 1673 | |
| FORD T | 1921 | B14 | BH 4081 | Wyatt, Yattendon |
| FORD T | 1922 | Healey B14 | DD 475 | |
| FORD T | 1926 | Fentiman B14 | BT 9420 | Fentiman, Seaton Ross |
| FORD TT | 1921 | | KK 980 | |
| GARDNER/ G.N.R. | 1941 | G.N.R. B35R | ZD 726 | Great Northern Rly. 324 |
| GILFORD Buda AS6 | 1931 | Eaton B20F | DX 9547 | Rivers, Ipswich |
| GILFORD Buda AS6 | | Willowbrook B20F | UT 7836 | Whelton, Coalville |
| GILFORD 1680T | 1931 | Weymann C30D | GW 713 | Valliant, Ealing |
| GILFORD 1680T | | Thurgood C34F | AG 8604 | Western S.M.T. |
| GILFORD 168SD | 1935 | Wycombe C26F | JR 3520 | |
| GILFORD 168MOT | 1932 | Wycombe C26F | JD 1981 | Hillman 112 |
| GUY Runabout | 1925 | | CD 9456 | Downland Cars, Brighton |
| GUY BTX | 1928 | Dodson O57R | DY 4965 | Hastings Tramways 3A |
| GUY Wolf | 1938 | Waveney B20F | JC 5313 | Llandudno |
| GUY Arab I | 1943 | Park Royal H56R | BFE 421 | Lincoln 66 |
| GUY Arab II | 1943 | Roe H56R | JTA 314 | Devon General DG 314 |
| GUY Arab II | 1944 | Park Royal H56R | FNY 933 | Pontypridd 37 |
| GUY Arab II | 1945 | Weymann H56R | HGC 130 | L.P.T.B. G351 |
| KARRIER E6 | 1934 | Brush H64R | TV 9333 | Nottingham 367 |
| KARRIER E4 | 1937 | Weymann H56R | CU 3593 | South Shields 204 |
| KARRIER W | 1945 | Roe H62R | CDT 636 | Doncaster 75 |
| KARRIER W | 1945 | Brush H56R | GTV 666 | Nottingham 466 |
| LEYLAND— | | | | |
|    G7 | 1922 | Short O51R | CD 7045 | Southdown 135 |
|    Lion PLSC1 | 1927 | Leyland B31F | KW 474 | Blythe & Berwick |
|    Lion PLSC1 | 1929 | Leyland B31F | J 4601 | J.M.T. 40 |
|    Lion PLSC3 | 1927 | Leyland B35F | KW 1961 | Blythe & Berwick |
|    Lion PLSC3 | 1928 | Short B35R | RP 5979 | United Counties L28 |
|    Lion PLSC3 | 1929 | Leyland B35R | RP 6946 | United Counties L63 |
|    Lion PLSC3 | 1929 | Leyland B30F | RU 8678 | Hants & Dorset 268 |
|    Lion LT1 | 1929 | Applewhite B30R | VL 1263 | Lincoln 5 |
|    Lion LT1 | 1929 | Leyland B35F | BR 7132 | Sunderland 2 |

| Chassis Type | Date | Body Details | Reg. No. | Original Owner |
|---|---|---|---|---|
| LEYLAND— | | | | |
| Lion LT1 | 1930 | Roe B30F | TF 818 | Lancashire United 202 |
| Lion LT2 | 1931 | Burlingham C31F | DV 7890 | Devon General 15 |
| Lion LT5A | 1934 | Leyland B34R | TJ 6760 | Lytham St. Annes 24 |
| Lion LT7 | 1935 | Massey B32R | ATD 683 | Widnes 39 |
| Lion LT7C | 1936 | Leyland B34R | BTB 928 | Lytham St. Annes 34 |
| Lion LT7C | 1937 | Leyland B34F | BTF 24 | Lytham St. Annes 44 |
| Lion LT8 | 1939 | Leyland B39F | JK 8418 | Eastbourne 12 |
| Lion LT8 | 1939 | Leyland B39F | JK 8421 | Eastbourne 15 |
| Titan TD1 | 1928 | E.C.O.C. L53R | JUB 29 | Wallace Arnold |
| | | originally ⎧ GE 2407 | | (chassis) Glasgow 72 |
| | | ⎩ YG 2058 | | (body) W. Yorkshire K 451 |
| Titan TD1 | 1929 | Brush O51R | UF 4813 | Southdown 813 |
| Titan TD1 | 1929 | Leyland L51ROS | DR 4902 | Southern National 2849 |
| Titan TD1 | 1929 | Leyland L51ROS | WH 1553 | Bolton 53 |
| Titan TD1 | 1930 | Leyland L48R | LJ 2941 | Hants & Dorset E 354 |
| Titan TD1 | 1931 | Leyland L48R | J 1199 | J.M.T. 24 |
| Titan TD2 | 1931 | Short H50R | UF 7428 | Southdown 928 |
| Titan TD2 | 1932 | Leyland H51R | J 6332 | J.M.T. 25 |
| Titan TD3 | 1934 | East Lancs H54R | AUF 670 | Southdown 970 |
| Titan TD3 | 1934 | English Electric O56R | AFY 971 | Southport 143 |
| Titan TD4 | 1936 | E.C.W. L55R | JG 8201 | East Kent |
| Titan TD4 | 1936 | Leyland O56R | JK 5605 | Eastbourne 95 |
| Titan TD4 | 1936 | E.C.W. L55R | BRM 596 | Cumberland 132 |
| Titan TD4 | 1937 | Leyland H56R | DLU 400 | L.P.T.B. STD90 |
| Titan TD4 | 1937 | Leyland H56R | ZC 714 | Dublin United R1 |
| Titan TD4 | 1937 | Brush L55R | ABL 766 | Thames Valley 336 |
| Titan TD4C | 1937 | Leyland H54R | BTF 25 | Lytham St. Annes 45 |
| Titan TD5 | 1938 | Leyland O56R | EFJ 241 | Exeter 26 |
| Titan TD5 | 1938 | Weymann H54R | FKO 223 | Maidstone & District 293 |
| Titan TD5 | 1939 | Weymann O58R | FEL 215 | Bournemouth 15 |
| Titan TD5 | 1940 | Park Royal H54R | GCD 48 | Southdown 248 |
| Titan TD7C | 1940 | M.C.W. H54C | HF 9126 | Wallasey 74 |
| Titan TD7 | 1940 | Leyland L53R | JP 4712 | Wigan 70 |
| Titan TD7 | 1941 | Roe H56R | BFE 419 | Lincoln 64 |
| Titan TD7 | 1942 | Roe H58C | EF 7380 | West Hartlepool 36 |
| Tiger TS2 | 1929 | Manchester B—R | VR 5996 | Manchester 33 |
| Tiger TS2 | 1929 | Duple C33F | DF 8420 | Black & White 37 |
| Tiger TS4 | 1932 | Santus B—R | EK 8867 | Wigan 81 |
| Tiger TS6T | 1936 | Leyland B39F | ATF 477 | Singleton, Leyland |
| Tiger TS7 | 1935 | Burlingham B35F | FW 5696 | Lincolnshire 368 |
| Tiger TS7 | 1935 | Burlingham B35F | FW 5698 | Lincolnshire 370 |
| Tiger TS7 | 1935 | Willowbrook B35R | BAL 610 | East Midland B10 |
| Tiger TS7 | 1936 | Windover C37F | JA 5515 | North Western |
| Tiger TS7 | 1937 | Harrington C32R | DUF 179 | Southdown 1179 |
| Tiger TS7 | 1937 | Harrington C32R | DKT 16 | Maidstone & District 558 |
| Tiger TS8 | 1938 | Park Royal C32F | JG 9956 | East Kent |

| Chassis Type | Date | Body Details | Reg. No. | Original owner |
|---|---|---|---|---|
| LEYLAND— | | | | |
| Tiger TS8 | 1938 | Weymann B35F | FEH 832 | P.M.T. 130 |
| Tiger TS8 | 1938 | Craven B32R | EFJ 666 | Exeter 66 |
| Tiger TF | 1939 | L.P.T.B. B34F | FJJ 774 | L.P.T.B. TF77 |
| Lioness PLC1 | 1927 | C26F | YT 3738 | King George V |
| Lioness LTB1 | 1929 | Burlingham C26D | DM 6228 | White Rose, (Rhyl) 7 |
| Cheetah LZ2 | 1936 | Santus B35F | NMY 556 | Webster, Wigan |
| Cub SKP3 | 1931 | C26F | TV 4847 | Skill's, Nottingham |
| Cub KP3 | 1932 | Willowbrook C20F | JU 963 | |
| Cub KPZ | 1936 | Harrington C14F | CUF 404 | Southdown 4 |
| Cub SKPZ2 | 1936 | Park Royal C18F | CLX 548 | L.P.T.B. C111 |
| Cub KP3 | 1939 | L.P.T.B. B20F | FXT 120 | L.P.T.B. CR14 |
| Badger TA | 1930 | Plaxton B20F | KW 7604 | Bradford Education Committee |
| Bull TQ2 | 1935 | Burlingham B32F | AAX 27 | West Monmouth 13 |
| TB7 | 1938 | Leyland H70R | EXV 201 | L.P.T.B. 1201 |
| TB7 | 1939 | Leyland H70R | EXV 253 | L.P.T.B. 1253 |
| TB7 | 1939 | Leyland H70R | EXV 348 | L.P.T.B. 1348 |
| MAXWELL | 1922 | Ch14 | CJ 5052 | |
| MORRIS-COMMERCIAL | 1927 | Bracebridge T | FU 7556 | F. Fox, Skegness |
| MORRIS-COMMERCIAL Dictator | 1932 | M.C.W. B32 | RB 55XX (It was one of a batch of 6 starting with these 2 numerals). | Chesterfield |
| MORRIS-COMMERCIAL | 1935 | | WV 8628 | |
| MORRIS-COMMERCIAL | 1935 | | CKE 64 | |
| N.G.T. SE6 | 1934 | Short B44F | CN 6100 | Northern General 604 |
| RANSOMES, SIMS & JEFFERIES | 1926 | R.S.J. B31D | DX5609 | Ipswich 8 |
| RANSOMES, SIMS & JEFFERIES | 1926 | R.S.J. B31D | DX 5617 | Ipswich 16 |
| RANSOMES, SIMS & JEFFERIES | 1929 | R.S.J. B31D | DX 7683 | Ipswich 41 |
| RANSOMES, SIMS & JEFFERIES | 1930 | R.S.J. B31D | DX 8871 | Ipswich 44 |
| REO Speed Wagon | 1924 | C14F | MR 3879 | |
| REO Gold Crown | 1931 | Economy B20F | AG 6740 | |
| REO Pullman | 1931 | Taylor C26F | NG 1109 | |
| RIKER | 1921 | O—R | NN 373 | |
| S.O.S. DON | 1935 | Brush B35F | RC 2721 | Trent 321 |
| STRAKER-CLOUGH | 1924 | Brush H50ROS | WT 7105 | Keighley 9 |
| SUNBEAM MS2 | 1935 | Park Royal H56D | ALJ 973 | Bournemouth 99 |

| Chassis Type | Date | Body Details | Reg. No. | Original Owner |
|---|---|---|---|---|
| SUNBEAM MS2 | 1935 | Park Royal O69R | ALJ 986 | Bournemouth 112 |
| SUNBEAM W | 1944 | Weymann H56R | RC 8472 | Derby 172 |
| SUNBEAM W | 1944 | Roe H62R | GKP 511 | Maidstone 56 |
| SUNBEAM W | 1945 | Park Royal H56R | RC 8575 | Derby 175 |
| THORNYCROFT | 1919 | Wadham O34R | BK 2986 | Portsmouth 10 |
| THORNYCROFT A2 Long | 1929 | Strachan & Brown B20F | UY 6596 | Worcester College for the Blind |
| THORNYCROFT 3-Axle | 1930 | | KF 1040 | Liverpool |
| TILLING-STEVENS Petrol Electric | 1923 | N.C.M.E. B | MN 2615 | Douglas |
| TILLING-STEVENS B49A7 | 1932 | Beadle B—R | JY 124 | Western National 3379 |
| TILLING-STEVENS Express | 1929 | ? B—R | DX 7812 | Eastern Counties |
| VAUXHALL Cadet VY | 1933 | Mount Pleasant B9 | OD 5489 | Bidgood Arms, Rockbeare |

*N.B.*—Several of the above were at one time in the fleet of J.M.T. and therefore bore Jersey registrations, viz.:—

| Mainland | Jersey | | Mainland | Jersey |
|---|---|---|---|---|
| DM 6228 | J 2975 | | NMY 556 | J 8545 |
| TF 818 | J 4229 | | BR 7132 | J 9008 |
| KW 474 | J 6825 | | CTW 210 | J 11668 |
| KW 1961 | J 7278 | | CUF 404 | J 13892 |
| YT 3738 | J 8462 | | | |

# INDEX